# Praise for *Hoop Dreams in Europe*

### Mike Barber
### *Richmond Times-Dispatch*

"It isn't the NBA or bust for American college players looking to make their living playing professional basketball. Finding a team, and sometimes a home, in a foreign country has been the path for many a former NCAA star. Himself a seasoned world traveler and vivid sports storyteller, David Driver takes us along for the adventure as these ballers keep hooping across the ocean in an effort to never give up their dribble. Driver serves up the flavor – on and off the court – of what life playing internationally is really all about in a book any fan of basketball or travel will enjoy."

*Mike Barber has spent the past 20 years*
*covering college athletics in Virginia.*

### Balázs Lipóczki
### Press Officer, Hungarian Basketball Federation

"The One Constant in the ever-changing World of Foreign Basketball in Hungary - that's David."

# HOOP DREAMS
## IN EUROPE

### AMERICAN BASKETBALL PLAYERS
### BUILDING CAREERS OVERSEAS

Lauren —
Hope to include
you in my
next Book on
Va. Basketball !
Dad

David S. Driver

*Credits*

**Front cover**
top left: Photo by David Driver of Damian Hollis (George Washington University) in Hungary
top right: Courtesy of NKE-Csata of Hungary of Kelley Austria (University of Dayton)
bottom left: Courtesy of Ferrol in Spain of Taylor Koenen (University of North Carolina)
bottom right: Courtesy of Hungarian Basketball of Ronald Curry (James Madision University)

**Back cover**
upper left: Photo by Liz Driver
bottom right: Photo courtesy of Kirby Burkholder, in Paris
bottom left: Photo by David Driver of press passes from Hungary

**Map illustrations**
Peter Hermes Furian, stock.adobe.com

**Design**
Front and back cover: Russell Nemec
Interior layout: Augusta Free Press LLC

Copyright © 2022 by David Driver

ISBN: 978-1-7923-8571-1

This book was printed in the United States of America.

*To Liz, who has brought joy and adventure
to my life on both sides of The Pond*

# Table of Contents

# Europe: 18 years, 18 countries

It was late fall of 2003, and for the first time in my life, I was headed in person to watch a professional sporting event in Europe. Inside the arena, on the Buda side of the Danube River on a cold night in Budapest, a men's basketball game was set to start. Instead of a crowd of about 16,000 – the average attendance at several NBA games I had covered in Washington as a stringer for the Associated Press – there were just a few hundred people in the stands of an arena that looked more like a high school gymnasium than a venue for a professional team.

After nearly 20 years of covering sports at all levels in the United States, I was about to chronicle a pro basketball game in a formerly communist country that, in terms of sports, was known more for its excellence in fencing and water polo.

The trip that took me to Budapest that day from the town in Hungary where I was living – Szeged, the paprika capital with a population of about 180,000 near the Serbian border – took about two hours. But it was a decade in the making.

In the early 1990s, not long after my wife, Liz, had finished a master's degree in linguistics, she and I took a train from Washington to New York City for her to interview for a job teaching English in Barcelona, Spain. She was offered the position. In the end, however, after some hard thinking, and even though it was exciting to think about being in Barcelona just before the Summer Olympics arrived in 1992, she turned down the job.

There was no one particular reason why we turned down a chance to move to Spain. The difficult decision somehow seemed right at the time ... or so we thought. And then life happened.

Skip ahead to 2003: – by then we had two daughters, Katie, age 11, and Dani, age 9, and Liz had just finished her doctorate in English literature from the University of Maryland. We were both looking for new challenges, as I had spent about 10 years as the sports editor of the weekly paper in Laurel, Maryland.

Liz learned of an opportunity to fill in for a professor at the University of Szeged, Hungary, while he would be spending the 2003-2004 academic year in the U.S.

Liz had spent a semester in Europe as an undergrad while in college at Eastern Mennonite University in Harrisonburg, Virginia, and as returning there to live for an extended period was on her to-do list. She made a quick exploratory visit, took a tour of the university and the town, discovered rehearsals underway for

Hungarian-language production of Shakespeare's Richard III in Szeged's famous summer arts festival in the town's huge cathedral square, and decided that she, and we, were in.

No one in our family knew a soul in Szeged; the only thing I knew about anything even remotely tied to Hungary was that my boyhood hero, New York Jets quarterback Joe Namath, had Hungarian roots. I remember watching Monday Night Baseball in the 1970s and the antics of reliever Al Hrabosky, known in the U.S. as the Mad Hungarian for his not-far-from insane behavior on the mound while trying to lock down a save in the ninth inning for the St. Louis Cardinals. Apart from those, I had nothing. (Years later, I was able to meet Al several times at Nationals Park in Washington as he worked as a broadcaster covering the Cardinals).

I was along for the ride as the trailing spouse. I had no idea what I would do professionally.

Turns out I had plenty to do in Hungary. The language is famous for its difficulty, and just trying to figure out how to live in another country took up mental and physical energy. We put our daughters into a regular Hungarian school, and it was my job to get them to and from that building on the south side of Szeged every day and normally have supper ready in the evening.

With my mornings free, I became friends with eurobasket.com, a website that tracks pro basketball leagues all over the world. Before leaving the States, I had contacted an American who took his basketball career overseas after playing in college at Bucknell University to ask about his experience and what it was like to live overseas. He was the first person I had talked to who had gone across the ocean to play pro basketball, and I really had no clue how it all worked.

How often are games played? How much money do American players make? What do foreigners do when they aren't at practice? How do they deal with a new culture and new language? These were all questions I would eventually ask of American men and women who went to Europe to play pro basketball.

Some of what I learned was that American men with NCAA Division I experience could earn six figures per season in top Western European leagues in France, Spain and Italy. And what happened after their careers were over? Many returned to become college assistant coaches in the United States, such as Craig Ponder, who played in Reading, England, and is now an assistant at the University of North Carolina Wilmington, and Eric Atkins, who played in college at Notre Dame, then in Greece and is now an assistant at George Washington.

I also learned that American athletes can be targets of unruly fans overseas. After a game I covered outside of London at Thames Valley, local Brits who perhaps had too much to drink got into a shouting match with some members of the home team, including Americans. Many European clubs have small cafes/ bars adjacent to the court where fans can mingle before, during and after games. Normally this is harmless, but on this night in England, it almost led to blows between players and drunken Brits.

More seriously, in November 2021, a man in Cyprus was arrested on attempted murder charges following an attack outside of a nightclub in the capital city, Nicosia, that left pro player Corey Manigault with brain injuries and on a ventilator for a time. Manigault who grew up in Maryland and played in college at Pitt and New Mexico, was averaging nearly 26 points per game in Cyprus at the time of the attack. His mother, in early December, told a television station in Washington, D.C. that her son was out of the ICU overseas. He played at Paul VI High in Fairfax, Virginia.

Fortunately, I didn't witness anything so horrific in my time in Europe.

During my first year in Europe, I was able to track down some of the roughly 20 American men who were playing pro hoops in Hungary in 2003-04. Some clubs couldn't afford these players – most of whom had played Division I ball. Other teams had at least two imports, and these players were normally expected to carry the scoring load for their teams. Sometimes when I attended games, it felt like I was watching a two-on-two contest with the four Americans on the court handling the ball the majority of the time.

Since Szeged's team was in Hungary's B League for men, the team couldn't afford any North Americans, that meant going north one hour to a city, Kecskemét, to see A-League ball. This city of about 110,000 is known for its apricot brandy and being the birthplace of a prominent 20th century composer, Zoltan Kodály.

But I was going there for the basketball.

Even that one-hour trip was an adventure. We didn't have a car - and didn't want one - while living in Hungary, so we had to rely almost solely on the train. Trains left Szeged for Kecskemét almost hourly. I would take one that allowed me to arrive early for the game, which usually began at 6 p.m. I approached some American players at courtside for an interview, and many times had made connections with them via e-mail to let them know I was coming. If I had time before the last train left for Szeged, I would interview American players after the game or follow up with them on the phone.

I began to pitch stories on some of the American players to newspapers, alumni magazines and Division I leagues, such as the Richmond, Virginia-based Colonial Athletic Association, and I was on my way. One of the first stories I wrote was on Chad McClendon, an all-Southern Conference player at Appalachian State University in the 1990s. After playing in Finland, Latvia, Israel, Lebanon and Spain, McClendon played several years in Hungary. I did a feature on him for Appalachian Today, the alumni magazine for ASU. I found that editors of many alumni magazines in the U.S. had a genuine interest in Americans playing overseas, and also what life was like away from the court.

As our girls got older, I ventured by train once a month or so to the neighboring countries of Austria, Slovakia, Slovenia and Serbia to track down and interview Americans who had made the trek to Europe to play pro basketball.

The trips to games were sometimes more eventful than the games themselves. I normally tried to get into town the day before a game, after trying (most of the time) to reach the American player by email to confirm when and where the game would be played. One Friday, however, I was walking down a street in the scenic town of Gmunden, Austria, when I saw a message board that said in English, "Basketball Tonight." I had been told the game was slated for the next day, so I quickly grabbed a taxi for the short drive to the arena and was able to interview several Americans after the game.

The nickname of the Gmunden team was the Swans, since a scenic lake sits in the middle of the town. We didn't have a lot of spending money at the time, but that weekend, I treated myself to two nights at a bed and breakfast in Gmunden. Snow on the ground, and the train ride from Szeged to Budapest to Vienna to, finally, Gmunden was magical – a sea of white outside the windows the entire trip.

A trip to Belgrade, Serbia, wasn't quite so magical. The first night I covered a game at Partizan Arena in the capital city, there were at least 200 armed policeman outside with face shields. During the previous game at the arena, some people had gotten injured when fans threw firecrackers (yes, indoors). After all that, I pointed out to some of my American friends that the Duke-North Carolina rivalry had nothing on any basketball showdown between Serbian and Croatian teams.

It had actually taken me a while to work up the nerve to cover a game in Belgrade, what with the NATO bombings from the 1990s still fresh in the psyche of Serbians. Most times, I went on my own. But in 2007, for U-19 world championships, I took my older daughter along so she could ready the maps while I drove. And there are many Hungarians in northern Serbian, no her language skills came in handy as well.

After watching the U.S. team practice, my daughter and I walked through the streets with these tall men from the gymnasium to a nearby restaurant for a reception. It was there I said hello for the first and only time to a young guard from Davidson College in North Carolina – one Steph Curry. He was very gracious even before I told him that I had covered his father, Dell, at Virginia Tech after the elder Curry had starred at a high school in Virginia that was one my school's rivals. I had played baseball in high school at Turner Ashby against Fort Defiance, the alma mater of Dell.

On another trip to Belgrade, I went with an American friend who was studying in Szeged, and he had gone to the hotel bar while I was at the game. He told me he spent the evening chatting with the locals, including a Serbian policeman who was proud to show off his gun.

I was happy to have slept through that after getting back from the game.

For the most part, covering pro basketball games was easier than trying to learn the Hungarian or Serbian languages. I tried to do that the best I could in Europe, even with the language barriers and limited technology in the early part of this century.

In Hungary, I made a business card that had a picture of a basketball, said in English and Hungarian that I was a sports journalist and that my address in Szeged. I just flashed that card – while saying "Good evening" and "I am a journalist" in my awful Hungarian – and I would be waved on through at the entrance.

Our family had originally planned to stay only one academic year in Hungary, but the university was so pleased with my wife's work that they found a spot for her once the Hungarian professor returned from the U.S. in 2004.

We ended up spending three academic years in Szeged. Our family traveled to Austria, Romania, Poland, Serbia, Croatia, Italy, the Czech Republic, Slovenia and other countries, and sometimes I would combine those trips with a chance to meet American basketball players.

All of the chapters listed are countries that I have been to, and in nearly every country, I was able to cover a pro basketball game or interview at least one American player.

After returning from Hungary in 2006, I have been able to make several return trips to that country as well as a trip to Belgium in 2016; a visit to Russia, Poland, Germany and Portugal during the 2018-19 season while my wife had teaching assignments in Russia and Hungary; and a two-week trip in October 2021 to Spain, where I was able to cover two women's games in the top league there and also visit a practice for the men's team in Seville.

During the latest trip, I was able to cover two women's games and interview University of Minnesota graduate Leslie Knight, who has played in Spain for nearly a dozen years, and Taylor Koenen, a 2020 graduate of the University of North Carolina in Chapel Hill who played in Switzerland her first pro year before moving to Spain for the 2021-22 season. Knight is featured on the back cover of this book while Koenen is on the front.

The afterword includes the latest information about the 2021-22 season on the challenges that American men and women face when playing overseas. I hope you enjoy your journey through Europe in the pages that follow, with stories from American ballers from all corners of the U.S.

# From Baltimore to Budapest

*This story originally ran in The Washington Times in 2019 and was reprinted by permission.*

Budapest — Growing up in Baltimore, Nick Faust knew basketball was going to take him places. The former Maryland Terrapins guard, who played three seasons in College Park under Mark Turgeon, just didn't know at the time the game would literally take him around the globe.

Since transferring and playing his senior year at Long Beach State, the 6-foot-5 forward has spent time in Israel, Italy and now Hungary, where he is trying to forge an identity as a go-to scorer with Atomeromu SE. The team is located in Paks, a town about 70 miles south of Budapest.

The Hungarian A league has 14 teams, and the number of foreigners it employs depends on the financial resources of the individual club. Faust is one of two Americans on his team, while Alba, a club in western Hungary, had five Americans on its recent roster.

Paks has been a stepping stone for other Americans from the District and surrounding areas, including former George Washington University standout Chris Monroe. A product of Good Counsel High in Montgomery County, Monroe was an all-star in Hungary and played in several European countries during a European pro career from 2003-13.

Less than three years out of college, Faust, 25, said the biggest difference between college basketball and the European leagues is the level of maturity and professionalism he has found overseas.

"College is talented kids playing basketball," Faust said. "Europe is grown men playing basketball — amateurism versus professionalism."

A lot depends on the country, of course. "Certain countries are more up to date with style of play in the game of basketball today," Faust said. "Whereas some countries are still a little bit behind."

But in Hungary, "life's amazing," he said. "Can't complain. Every day is a new destiny."

For him, the game has never felt like a job. "My whole life I've never had a (regular) job and still don't," Faust said. "I love what I do."

In his first year as a pro in 2016-17 Faust was an all-star in an Israeli league, and then spent part of last season with a team in Italy.

Faust is not the only former Maryland hoopster playing this winter in Hungary. Former women's star Shatori Walker, who played for the Washington Mystics in 2018, averaged 16.7 points per contest in her first 11 games for Miskolc in the top Hungarian women's league.

"The main difference that is the most noticeable for me is the physicality," Walker wrote in an email earlier this month. "In the NCAA, there's a one-touch rule when the offensive players are protected a lot more."

In his first 13 games this season in Hungary, Faust has averaged 13.2 points per contest. On Dec. 30, Faust started and scored 13 points, with a trio of 3-pointers in Atomeromu SE's win over KTE-Duna Aszfalt before a crowd of about 800 fans in Paks.

The former Baltimore prep star said he had no second thoughts about leaving the Terrapins program after the 2013-14 season — a year in which Turgeon suffered several defections.

"I'm happy with every decision I have ever made in my life," Faust said. "I wouldn't change a thing. Don't get me wrong: it was fun at the University of Maryland. I always respect the University of Maryland. I just wanted to better myself."

After sitting out a year due to NCAA rules, Faust nearly doubled his scoring average to 17.4 points per game at Long Beach State.

"God is continuing to bless my family and at the end of the day, that's all that matters," he said. "God just wanted the world to see me, literally."

*Update: Faust averaged 14 points per game for a team in Poland in 2020-21. Walker-Kimbrough was scoring more than 21 points for a team in Israel in games through early December.*

# From Dayton to Hungary for Austria

*This story originally ran in the alumni magazine of the University of Dayton in 2019 and was reprinted by permission.*

Budapest — In her last season with the Flyers, guard Kelley Austria '17 contemplated playing pro basketball overseas. That her successful college career was injury-plagued, however, made Austria wary of such global — and challenging — goals.

But the Ohio native has not only been able to reach such heights but also has been able to see parts of the world that are outside the realm of possibility for many Americans. And it's not lost on Austria that pro basketball careers overseas are not as abundant for American women as they are for men.

"When I was young, my dream was to be a professional basketball player; it's a blessing to have the opportunity to do that," said Austria, who was averaging 8.5 points and 1.5 assists in her first 11 Hungarian league games this season.

Not only is Austria getting to play basketball for a living, but her first two seasons overseas have taken her to tourist hot spots in Greece and now Budapest.

"Last season I played for Niki Lefkada, a team on an island in Greece. Greece is probably the most beautiful place I have ever been," she said. "I'm hoping to have a little off time this season to travel and explore other countries in Europe."

Hungary, a country of about 10 million people, is about the size of Indiana. Under Communist rule through the late 1980s, it joined the European Union in 2004. Austria has been able to see some of the notable sites in Budapest, including Buda Castle, Castle Hill, St. Stephen's Basilica and Heroes' Square.

"When we get free time I'll watch a lot of Netflix, and I'll go to a cafe with the other American on the team, walk around fashion street or the square, or try and find a new place for lunch or dinner. Sometimes we will have team get-togethers on our off days," Austria said.

"I think the biggest difference in style I have noticed is how much more physical the game is here in Europe. You can get away with things that would definitely be called fouls in college.

"A little challenge I face is the language barrier. Most of the time the coach is speaking and coaching in Hungarian — which can be nice at times because when he is yelling at us I have no idea what he is saying — but thankfully a player on the team is always translating for the Americans."

Although the Hungarian language is particularly hard for English speakers to learn, nearly every team in Europe has at least one player who speaks English.

"My agent is Hungarian, so he is very familiar with all the teams here. He told me that NKE Csata was interested in me, so I learned more about the team and the city they are in and decided to sign to play with them," Austria said.

"All my days are very similar," she added. "I usually always have one practice a day; and two to three times a week, I'll have morning practice or weights as well as the evening practice. The days can get a little boring, so on off days I try to get out of my apartment and explore a little. The biggest adjustment for me is learning how to live on my own. Living in a different country has been challenging, but it has also been a great experience."

Austria grew up in Beavercreek, Ohio, and helped UD win Atlantic 10 regular-season titles in 2013 and 2014. She was the A-10 defensive player of the year as a senior in 2017.

"I wouldn't be where I am today in my basketball career if it wasn't for my dad," she said "He taught me the game and has been training and coaching me since I was in fourth grade. I'm grateful for all his time and all the sacrifices he's made to help me make my basketball dreams become a reality. I've also had great coaches throughout my basketball career that have challenged me and pushed me to become a better basketball player and get to the professional level.

*Update: Austria last played in Hungary during the 2018-19 season. Former Dayton standout Samantha McCay, whose college career with the Flyers ended in 2013, has played for several years in Greece after earlier stops in Hungary, France and Latvia.*

# Michigan State Product Grew Up a Hoosier

*This story originally ran in the Kokomo Tribune in 2014 and was reprinted by permission.*

Székesfehérvár, Hungary — Sometimes Brandon Wood is easy to spot in this city of about 100,000 people in western Hungary, as he maneuvers his new Fiat 500L around town.

His basketball team, Alba Fehervar, provides him the free use of the car along with an apartment above the Vodafone Sportcentrum and a daily meal allowance in addition to his monthly salary. The cars stand out since even non-hoop fans are aware of the team.

But Kokomo High product Wood is also hard to miss when he walks down the streets of one of the most historic cities in a country about the size of Indiana and one under the Communist orbit until about 25 years ago.

Wood is one of the few African-Americans in this city — or the country. In fact, Wood said he can't remember running into another American in his first weeks here in this city this fall. But that doesn't dissuade his enjoyment of life as a pro hoopster in Europe.

"It is easy being over here for me," said guard Wood, 25, sitting in a hotel restaurant the morning after his team lost at home to fall to 3-3 overall in mid-November as his Romanian head coach offered his resignation after the game. "I can relate to all different kinds of people. I know how to speak and carry myself.

That is a skill that people I know could not do.

"Of course, all eyes are on you because there are not many of us," he added. "I have not had any issues off the court. A lot of stares but a lot of love, really."

Wood said his background growing up prepared him for life in Europe. His team this season has included several Hungarians, Serbians and two Americans from Maryland: former DePaul player Cleveland Melvin and Lasan Kromah, who played last season for national champ UConn.

Wood was 7 when his family moved from Philadelphia to Howard County in Indiana.

"When I was going to middle school, most of my friends were from the country," said Wood, who attended Northwestern and played baseball, basketball and football. "Most of my friends were white."

He then attended Kokomo High. "When I moved into the city I got exposed to different cultures," said Wood, comparing that experience to a smaller Philadelphia.

Wood is living in Hungary with his wife, Aujalen Aldridge, who is from Alabama and met Wood when she was living in Marion. They were married on July 15; Aujalen, who is also African-American, studied nursing at the University of Phoenix and is working on developing a line of perfume.

"I get a lot of stares. It doesn't bother me at all," said Aujalen, who chalks up the glances to the fact many Hungarians have not seen African-Americans in person.

Both of them come from military families. Aldridge spent part of her high school years at an American school in Germany and played some prep hoops.

What does she tell her family and friends back home about Hungary? "I just tell them literally everything is different, to the way you cut on the light [for electricity] to the food. Everything is like the opposite [of the United States], really," she said.

Aujalen said her time in Germany helped prepare for living in Europe as an adult. She joined Wood for a few weeks when he played last season in Italy.

"If you come over here for the first time and try to get adjusted it would be hard," she said.

Most European teams practice two times a day and play once a week, and that is the case in Hungary for Wood. Morning practice normally runs from 10 to 11:30 a.m. After that he will have lunch — provided for by the team — and then get some rest before evening practice from 5:30 to 7 p.m.

He and his wife enjoy watching television in the evening, and one favorite is a British show based on a modern-day Sherlock Holmes. This week, the couple stayed up late to watch Wood's former school Michigan State play Duke in a college basketball game from Indianapolis. The time difference between Hungary and the East Coast of the United States is six hours.

His team lifts weights together once a week but Wood has been lifting on his own every other day in recent months. "If the hardest thing I have to do is run and lift weights it is a pretty good life," he said.

The couple also spend time with a Hungarian woman who is a big fan of the team and also teaches English in her home. "We will get coffee when the team is on the road," Aujalen said.

Wood met the Hungarian teacher when he played for the team a few years ago and the couple will meet every few weeks with her young students so they can practice their English. "They will ask us how America is," said Wood, who averaged 15.5 points per game in the first four contests in Hungary this season.

Wood averaged 8.8 points per game as a senior for Michigan State in 2011-12 and then played for Albacomp here during the 2012-13 season as he averaged nearly 19 points per outing. He spent part of last season in Italy and then returned to Székesfehérvár after an opportunity to play in Austria fell through earlier this season.

Székesfehérvár has about 100,000 people and is among the 10 largest cities in the country located in central Europe. It is about 40 miles southwest of capital Budapest, which is home to about two million of the 10 million people in the land-locked country.

The Hungarian language is considered one of the hardest for non-native speakers to master and it is not related to any other languages in the region. "It is a difficult language. It is very hard," Aujalen said.

There are pockets of Hungarians who live in neighboring Slovakia to the north and Serbia to the south.

Székesfehérvár means "white castle of the [royal] seat" in English and 15 rulers are buried here, according to wikipedia.com. The basketball team has been one of the most successful in Hungary and normally has been able to afford the three foreign players who are allowed to suit up for one of the 14 teams in the top circuit in the country.

"We could not be any happier. I just feel so blessed to be in this position and do what I love every day and continue to play a game for a living. Not many people get to play for a living," Wood said. "Life here off the court has been great."

*Update: Wood later played in Italy, Macedonia, Lithuania, Switzerland, Greece and was in Mexico and Argentina during the 2019-20 season. Among the former Michigan State players who were in Europe this season were Kenny Goins and Marvin Clark, who were with different teams in Hungary, according to www. eurobasket.com*

# GW's Hollis Won Title

*This story originally ran on the website of George Washington University in 2014 and was reprinted by permission.*

Székesfehérvár — Damian Hollis ('10) got the basketball and drove down the lane for an acrobatic layup, sending the blue and white-clad home fans into a frenzy here in late May.

His basket gave his team a 10-point lead with 90 seconds left in the game to seal a playoff win, but the cheers that came down on the former GW standout were much different than the ones he experienced at the Smith Center in Foggy Bottom. The most noticeable change - those chants are in Hungarian, one of the more difficult languages for a foreigner to learn.

A four-year player for GW through 2010, Hollis recently finished his third season playing in the top pro league in this western Hungarian city of about 101,000 people just over an hour away west of capital Budapest. This city dates to around 997 A.D. and was the location for the crowning of many kings, while in modern times it has been home to champion football (soccer), ice hockey and basketball clubs.

Hollis had 13 points as Albacomp added to that legacy and won at home 75-66 in the deciding game of the best-of-five series on June 2 over visiting Szolnok. It was the first European title for Hollis, who is one of several former GW standouts who played for pay during the 2012-13 campaign and the third to win a league title in the last two seasons. Former GW star Pops Mensah-Bonsu won a title in Turkey in 2012 and Chris Monroe was part of a championship squad in Russia in 2013.

"I was ready to keep playing basketball and see where it took me," said the soft-spoken Hollis, standing outside the home locker room about one hour before Game 3 of the championship series in Hungary. "I knew I had a chance to be something across the water. I just didn't know where. I had to figure it out."

Some NCAA products without an NBA pedigree play in the D-League after their college career. That was not a consideration for Hollis, who pointed out top Division I products can make more money in Europe than the NBA feeder system.

"I definitely wanted to come to Europe. If anything, I wanted to experience Europe. It is priceless to be in Hungary, just down the street from Budapest," said the 6-foot-8 Hollis, whose uniform is filled with ads for team sponsors, which is typical in Europe.

Hollis did not head out to begin his pro career in Hungary. He got cut from a team in Belgium in his first season out of college and landed in Hungary, a country of about 10 million people about the size of Indiana that was under Communist rule until the late 1980s. Hungary, a world soccer power in the 1950s and 1960s, joined the European Union in 2004.

Albacomp has a passionate fan base that beats on drums and blows whistles when the opponent is at the foul line in the style of European soccer fans. Some fans wore blue and white scarfs in support of the team.

"It was rocking," said Hollis of the sellout crowd of 2,200 fans that were on hand during the Hungarian league finals. Among those in attendance at Game 3 was team president Kornel David, the first Hungarian to play in the NBA and a teammate with Michael Jordan in Chicago; and Adam Hanga, 24, a Hungarian who was drafted by the San Antonio Spurs in 2011 and played this past season in Spain, which has one of the top leagues in Europe.

Hollis, who averaged 13.9 points and 4.9 rebounds as a GW senior in 2009-10, nearly duplicated those numbers this season for Albacomp. He tallied about 13 points and six boards per contest and averaged nearly two assists and two steals.

"He is a great teammate. First and foremost, he is a great man," said guard Brandon Wood, a former Michigan State player who was teammates this season with Hollis. "He is just a fun person. He does a lot of things well on the court. He is a good all-around player."

"He is a very good guy. He played well for us," said Albacomp assistant coach Gabor Matus, who is Hungarian.

How did GW prepare Hollis for his pro career? "As far as basketball, being obedient and getting extra time in the gym. I definitely learned that from GW," he said.

A native of Fort Lauderdale on the east coast of Florida, Hollis - as is customary for top American players in Europe - was provided a free apartment and car with a meal allowance this past season in land-locked Hungary. He lived in a flat about a five-minute walk from the Vodafone Sportcentrum, tucked just off a tree-lined street a few minutes from a McDonald's and small family-owned stores.

"It has obviously been a change. I came from Fort Lauderdale and the beach is right down in Miami. Then I went to D.C., where there is always something to do. I have to find things to do with my time" in slower-paced Hungary, he said.

Hollis became a dual citizen of Hungary last fall and that means he does not count against the limit of only three North Americans allowed per team in Hungary. He tried to become a dual citizen of Hungary after first season with Albacomp. After delays it was written in his contract that a deadline would be set for him to get the proper paperwork late last year.

"It gives me a better and higher marketing value," Hollis said. "I am an American, obviously, but they don't use me as a foreigner since I am part of the European Union." The other Americans with Albacomp in the league finals were Wood, Ronald Moore (Siena) and Jarrod Jones (Ball State).

The former GW forward is no stranger to European basketball. His father, Essie, is a member of the sports Hall of Fame at St. Bonaventure and played pro hoops in Spain and one season with the Detroit Pistons.

The younger Hollis, who made trips to Spain with his father, played for the U.S. U-19 national team in the world championships in Serbia, which borders Hungary to the south, in 2007 following his freshman year for the Buff and Blue. The Americans lost in the gold medal game to host Serbia. His American teammates on that squad included Stephen Curry (Davidson), now a star in the NBA with Golden State.

"I was kind of used to him being open to the European culture," Hollis said of time spent with his father. "He spread that to me. It was not that tough of an adjustment as for other people. It is amazing to be able to play basketball for a living and be in this lifestyle."

## The Global Game

A list of several former GW basketball players who played overseas during the 2012-13 season, according to usbasket.com

Men
Robert Diggs - Iceland
Carl Elliott - Venezuela
Mike Hall - Israel
Damian Hollis - Hungary
Pops Mensah-Bonsu - Spain/Italy
Chris Monroe - Russia
Hermann Opoku - Austria
Danilo Pinnock - Puerto Rico

Women
Jessica Adair - Australia
Elisa Aguilar - Russia
Anna Montanana - Turkey/Spain
Elena Vishnyakova – France

*Update: Former GW standout Tyler Cavanaugh, who also played for Wake Forest, saw time for Atlanta and Utah in the NBA and later played in Spain and Germany, was averaging about 11 points per game in December of this season for his team in Lithuania. Japan native Yuta Watanabe, who ended his GW career in 2018, has played in the NBA for Memphis and Toronto. Former GW guard Tony Taylor, from Sleepy Hollow, New York, has played in Turkey, Russia, Poland, Italy and Turkey; he was averaging around 11 points and three assists per contest for his team in Turkey in mid-December. Monroe was the leading scorer in school history when he left and after a long career overseas returning to work in the athletic department at the Atlantic 10 Conference school.*

# Washington State Goes Wordly

*This story originally ran in the alumni magazine of Washington State in 2009 and was reprinted by permission.*

Szolnok — With more and more Europeans on the roster of NBA teams, Americans like Jan-Michael Thomas (class of 2001) have to look outside the United State if they want to continue their hoop careers.

As a Cougar basketball player, Jan-Michael Thomas ('01 Bus. Mgt.) was one of the top long-range shooters in the country. Now he's a lot farther than a three-point shot from his American roots.

Thomas spent this past basketball season playing for a pro team in Szolnok, Hungary, about an hour southeast of the capital, Budapest.

"It is a great country, in terms of basketball, for someone who wants to get the opportunity to play," says Thomas, a point guard who grew up near Los Angeles.

"They are real passionate about sports and life." That can be said about basketball fans throughout Europe.

With more and more Europeans on the roster of NBA teams, Americans such as Thomas have to look outside the United States if they want to continue their hoop careers. Teams overseas are willing to pay competitive prices-and provide free housing and transportation-to get Americans across the Atlantic.

Thomas, in fact, wanted to play overseas in the 2002-03 and 2003-04 seasons but was left without a job due to the tight market for imports. During that time he stayed in shape and had a small role in the movie, Coach Carter, which starred Samuel L. Jackson and was released January 2005.

Besides Thomas, several other former WSU players were with pro teams overseas at some point this past season: Tyrone Brown and Terrence Lewis, New Zealand; Mike Bush, Luxembourg; Chris Crosby '01, Norway; Carol Daniel, France; Isaac Fontaine '97, China; Cedrick Hughey and Jerry McNair, Mexico; Jay Locklier '01, Argentina; Kojo Bonsu-Mensah and David Vik, Portugal; Pawel Stasiak '03 Poland; and Ezenwa Ukeagu '04, Germany.

And at least one WSU graduate, Guy Williams, helps players hook up with teams overseas. A former Cougar and NBA player, Williams works for SportsTalent, an agency based in Washington State that represents players.

Crosby, Daniel, and Locklier have each played for pay in the minor leagues in the United States and several other countries. Locklier, who grew up in South Carolina and graduated with a degree in business, played in the National Basketball Development League (NBDL), a feeder system for the NBA.

"I would think some of the pluses are obvious," he says. "It is run by the NBA. There will be no problem getting your money. Plus, you will be playing in front of NBA scouts. It is kind of political. Everyone is out for themselves. It is not just players: coaches, trainers, referees, the front office-they all want to move up to the NBA."

So, what are the positives and negatives of playing overseas?

"I would say, first of all, it depends where you are," says Locklier, explaining that some countries pay on time and others do not. "It is a real-world education. You get to see a lot of places you normally would not see. The negative is being on the road eight or nine months a year, living out of a suitcase. We take a lot for granted here in the United States. If we say you get paid the first of the month, you get paid the first of the month. That is not always the case in some Europe leagues."

Locklier played last fall in Argentina, then returned to Pullman for the spring semester to pursue a master's degree in athletic administration. He hopes to play basketball this fall, but also plans to send out his resume for a "regular job" in athletic administration.

Crosby, who hails from Colorado, has been with pro teams in Portugal, Greece, Australia, and Norway and with minor league teams in the U.S.

"It's stressful," Crosby says of playing overseas. "The job stability . . . there is no job stability. But I have enjoyed it a lot. It has made me a better person. You have to understand people better. I feel so lucky to be 27 now and still be playing basketball."

While the NBDL pays around $25,000 per season, top Americans who play in Europe can make a lot more money, depending on the country and, of course, their ability and experience. NBA-caliber players can make at least $500,000 per season in countries such as Spain, Italy, and Greece. Top American players in Hungary can make nearly $100,000 per season.

And while Crosby was never drafted by the NBA, he says he made $4,500 per month, tax free. with a 10-month contract this past season in Norway. On top of that, he had a meal allowance that he figured was worth another $1,500 per month. So that works out to a season salary of about $60,000.

Daniel, another former Cougar from Colorado, has also made a living as a pro basketball player in the American minor leagues and overseas. Daniel has played with teams in France, Japan, the Philippines, Israel, and Australia. He ranked sixth in the Continental Basketball Association in rebounds this past season. He averaged 11.5 points and 7.8 boards per game for the Yakima Sun Kings after he began the 2004-05 season in France.

What are the positives and negatives of playing in the States instead of going abroad?

"Staying in the States, there is no language barrier, and you are close to home," Daniel says. "Financially, it becomes a lot harder" to make a living in North American minor leagues.

How did WSU prepare him for new cultures?

"Being in a small place like Pullman, you have to learn to fend for yourself. Overseas, you are isolated," Daniel says.

Nearly every male basketball player who begins his NCAA career at the Division I level, especially in a league like the Pac-10, has dreams of the NBA. But the laws of supply and demand are against him, especially with the influx of foreign players to the NBA. This past season there were more than 70 foreign-born players in the NBA from nearly 30 countries.

"There was never an opportunity [for me] as far as minor leagues in the States," Thomas says. "That is for people with big names. I knew I wanted to come to Europe. I wanted to travel and see the countries."

Who knows? He may be part of a large Cougar contingent in Europe in the upcoming season.

"I have no problem staying in Europe," Thomas says.

*Update: Among the former Washington State players overseas, per www. eurobasket.com, early this season were Ahmed Ali (Croatia), Mike Acquaah (Cyprus), Isaac Bonton (Lithuania), Charles Callison (Ukraine), Davante Cooper (Albania), Robert Franks (Australia), Josh Hawkinson (Japan), Taylor Rochestie (France), Brock Motum (France), DaVonte Lacy (Slovakia), Ike Iroegbu (Israel) and Xavier Thames (Hungary). Thames ended his college career at San Diego State and was drafted by Toronto in 2014. He was interviewed by the author at the Hungarian Cup in northwest Hungary in 2019. Lacy was among the top scorers in school history.*

# N.C. State's Chones Excelled in Europe

*This article first appeared on the website of the Washington Mystics in 2006 and was reprinted by permission.*

Szeged — Hungary, a country of 10 million people in central Europe, is known for its spicy paprika, the Danube River that flows through Budapest and being the homeland of American icons such as Zsa Zsa Gabor and Joe Namath.

Hungary also has a very strong women's basketball league, as Kaayla Chones of the Washington Mystics is learning. Chones is playing this winter season for BSE-ESMA Budapest, one of 11 teams in the top Hungarian women's league.

"I think it is little more physical than playing in the States," Chones said in a telephone interview Nov. 28 from her Budapest apartment. "I knew it was competitive and physical. I came prepared for that. I knew I had to be more aggressive."

"I am a post player. I am a center. My game has always been aggressive," she added. "It gives me a chance to be a leader on the team."

Chones, in her second season with the Mystics, appeared in 12 games in 2005 and averaged just 5.1 mpg, 1.2 ppg and 0.5 rpg.

She notes that she played behind several experienced and talented centers this past summer in Washington. Chones estimated that she is playing about 30 minutes per game in Hungary.

"I am ... dusting off my skills and getting ready for training camp," said the 6-foot-3 center, who turns 25 in January. "I am just trying to focus on being aggressive. I am such a young player."

Unlike the NCAA or WNBA, European leagues play 10-minute quarters. In international play, the three-second lane is a trapezoid, not a rectangle, wider at the basket end. Walking is called more quickly than in the NCAA and WNBA when a player does not clearly put the ball on the floor before she picks up her pivot foot.

Chones also has to adjust to a Hungarian coach, Sandor Farkas, who does not speak English. She said some of her Hungarian teammates who speak English translate some of his advice during a game. "If they remember," she added. "Basketball is basketball, world-wide. I have been here two months and it is getting easier."

Her team normally practices from 9:30 to 11 a.m. and again from 5:30 to 7 p.m. It is normal for European teams, both men's and women's, to practice twice a day during the week.

Chones has had several big games recently. She had 21 points and seven rebounds on Nov. 27 in a 75-67 loss to Zala Volan; she had 24 points and five rebounds Nov. 25 in a 116-51 win over BEAC; and she had 31 points and eight rebounds Nov. 13 in a 75-55 win over Raba.

Her team also plays in the tough Euroleague (against teams from outside Hungary), and in her first six games there she averaged 15.3 ppg, 6.3 rpg and 29 mpg. She made 40 of 65 shots from the field (61.5 percent), 12 of 21 from the line (57.1) and had seven assists, 13 steals and 13 turnovers.

Hungary was under Communist control until the early 1990s. The country is about the size of Indiana, and nearly 20 percent of the population lives in Budapest. There are very few other cities with a population more than 200,000 people.

Chones has been to Germany, Slovakia and Croatia with her team for EuroLeague games. On Thanksgiving Day, which is not celebrated in Hungary, her team played a game in Zagreb, Croatia.

Chones first came to Europe when she was 15, on a basketball trip to Belgium as part of a sports exchange program in her home state of Ohio. Chones plans to head home to States for the holidays on Dec. 22, then return to Hungary on Jan. 3 with an eye on preparing for Mystics' training game that begins in April.

*Update: Chones ended her overseas career in Israel in 2012-13. Another former North Carolina State product to play in Hungary was Chelsea Nelson, who was averaging nearly 16 points per game in December for PEAC; she is a native of Tennessee. Kiara Leslie, who began her college career at Maryland, was drafted out of North Carolina by Washington of the WNBA in the first round in 2019. She began this season in Israel after playing in Russia in 2020-21, according to www. eurobasket.com.*

# Hawaii to Hungary

*This story originally ran in the alumni magazine of Hawaii in 2006 and is reprinted by permission.*

Peter Kecskes, 26, spent just one academic year at the Univeristy of Hawaii at Manoa, but it was memorable. Sitting in an outdoor coffee shop in Szeged, Hungary, in June 2005, prior to the wedding of an American basketball teammate, the Hungarian reminisced.

"My family came out for Christmas. It was really a fun experience to not have snow on Christmas," he said. "To go on the beach on the 25th was pretty neat."

Just one of many non-Americans who haves been part of the Rainbow Warrior basketball program during the past several years, Kecskes is also among the former Hawaii basketball players who keep playing post-college by turning pro in Europe. He played last season for MAFC in his native Budapest and is spending the 2005–06 season with Nyíregyháza, in northeast Hungary.

Other former Rainbows who played overseas in 2004–2005 include Mindaugas Burneika (Russia), Paul Jesinskis (Finland), Troy Ostler (Belgium), Fabio Ribeiro (Brazil), Predrag Savovic (Spain), Haim Shimonovich (Israel), Luc Arthur Vebobe (France) and Ales Zivanovic (Lithuania). Former Rainbow Warrior Trevor Ruffin, an MVP in Europe, returned to his hometown this year to play for the Buffalo Rapids.

"Sometimes it gets discouraging because you don't think you're getting anywhere, but you have to keep your head up and keep playing hard and something will turn up," Ostler told the Honolulu Star-Bulletin in 2003.

It did. Ostler, who averaged 16 points per game for the Rainbows in 2000–01, scored about 10 points per game in Belgian league play last season. He parlayed his success in Belgium to a spot with Navigo in the A league in Italy, which has one of the top circuits in Europe.

Vebobe's team, Paris Basket Racing, played at home in southeast Paris last January. His team won 72-66 over Reims before a crowd of about 2,000 fans on a cold Saturday night. Basketball is very popular in France—at least five French men played in the NBA this past season, and a book about French pro basketball filled with color action photos can be found at a bookstore on one of the major tourist streets in Paris.

Burneika, who ended his college career in 2002, averaged 12.8 points per game last season for Spartak in Russia. After completing his Hawaii career in 2004, Jesinskis averaged nearly 6 points and 5 rebounds as a first-year pro.

Savovic, who averaged 20 points per game for the Rainbows in 2001–02, signed a two-year contract extension in June 2005 to remain in Spain. He was born in Pula, Croatia, a town of about 60,000 people located on the Adriatic Sea in the northwest part of the country. Pula was once part of Yugoslavia, a region familiar to UH hoops fans who've cheered for Milos Zivanovic of Belgrade (Serbia and Montenegro) the past four seasons.

Kecskes had planned to attend Wright State in Ohio, but the head coach there was fired, and the Hungarian big man ended up at Hawaii. He remembers his first visit.

"On the recruiting visit, they gave me all of the traditional meals—pork and chicken. They gave me all of that stuff," he says. He was a redshirt during the 1997–98 season at Hawaii and eventually earned a degree in computer science from a university in Budapest.

So how does Kecskes, who has played several pro seasons in Europe, compare NCAA Division I college hoops to the European pro circuit?

"It was tough. It is really more physical" in the United States, he says.

*Update: Former players with the Rainbows in Europe this season include Noah Allen, who was averaging nearly 12 points per game for a team in Palencia, Spain. He played earlier in Germany after an appearance in the summer league with the Washington Wizards in 2019. Garrett Nevels, who grew up in California, played in Poland and Portugal during the 2020-21 season and was with a team in Serbia this season.*

# Staying Loyal to Loyola

*This story originally ran in the Baltimore Examiner in 2006.*

Wels, Austria — It is not hard to spot Rod Platt when he walks into the train station in Wels, Austria. To begin with, the Loyola College graduate is about 6-foot-9. And Platt is an African-American in a central European country that is mostly white.

That is no big deal to big man Platt, who has played pro basketball in Austria for the past four seasons.

"That is the one thing I have always noticed: They are not as worried about things as they are back home," said Platt, in a recent telephone interview from Wels, a town with about 55,000 people. "They are laid-back and relaxed over here."

Platt graduated from Loyola in 1999 with a degree in philosophy. He then spent three seasons playing pro hoops in The Netherlands, then moved to WBC Wels in the top Austrian league prior to the 2002-03 season.

"Everyone can't make it to the NBA. I don't know if that is realistic anymore," said Platt, who was the Most Valuable Player of the Austrian All-Star game in 2004. "I am just going to play as long as I can."

Platt, 30, is one of several basketball players from Baltimore-area colleges who now makes his living as a pro hoopster overseas. Another is guard Fred Warrick, who finished his career at Coppin State in 1999. He has spent the past four seasons playing in the Czech Republic. Living overseas is not easy, no matter the line of work.

"The most challenging? I guess being away from my family, being away from my son," said Warrick, whose 6-year-old son lives in Washington.

Warrick is provided the free use of an apartment and a car in the Czech

Republic. He is less than four hours from Prague, which Warrick calls his favorite city in Europe.

Tom Martin, who played in college at Towson University from 1987-89, has played overseas for nearly 10 years. He is a guard this season in London.

"When I first go to London, teams were only allowed two Americans per team," Martin wrote in an e-mail from England. "Today, most teams play with five foreign players. The need to get better has seen the rise in young, talented (European) players. I run my own basketball clinic in schools and colleges, and next year I am going to offer trips to a U.S. basketball camp for one or two of my young prospects."

Another Towson product, Baltimore's Kurk Lee, played several years in Finland.

The European season lasts until May, and sometimes June. Most teams play just one game per week, which gives American imports a lot of free time. Many European teams practice in the morning, take the afternoon off, then practice again in the early evening. Leagues in western Europe allow at least three Americans per team. Hungary allows just two Americans per team, while several teams in Romania and Serbia have one or no Americans on the roster.

"I use free time to see sights, interact with vasts amount of people from different cultures," Martin wrote. He added that he enjoys dining out, and adds the club scene in London is "vibrant and fun."

Most top Americans in Europe can earn at least six figures per season, and most of the time their salaries are tax-free. American imports in central Europe can make nearly $100,000 per season, while NBA-caliber players in countries such as Spain, Italy and France can make at least $500,000 per season.

John Gilchrist received a lot of attention after he left the Maryland Terps after his junior season in 2004-05. This year, as a first-year pro for Maccabi Rishon Le-Zion in Israel, he averaged 14.5 points and 30.5 minutes per game in his first 17 contests.

Tamir Goodman, who played at Towson, has played pro ball in Israel for several years.

Warrick, 29, held the single-game scoring record of 49 points for the Czech league until it was broken by fellow American Adam Hess during the 2004-05 season. Hess played at William & Mary. Warrick is related to Maurice Whitfield (Norfolk State), who has played in the Czech Republic the past few seasons.

The style of play in Europe is unlike that of the NCAA. There are a few basic rule differences between Europe and top-level American leagues. The game in Europe has 10-minute quarters, the ball can be touched once it hits the rim, the three-second lane is a trapezoid and thus wider near the basket, and a player is called for walking if he does not clearly put the ball on the floor before he picks up his pivot foot.

Martin wrote that getting used to the walking call was a big adjustment on the court in Europe.

"The game is a little different," Warrick said. "There are a lot of mainly shooters here, and they are a lot more fundamentally sound" than most American players.

The Global Game
Here is a look at male basketball players from local colleges who have played pro basketball overseas this 2005-06 season:
• Coppin State: Pierre-Yves Denervaud (Switzerland), Julian King (Paraguay), Terquin Mott (Venezuela), Dorian Pena (Phillipines), Rafi Reavis (Phillipines), Larry Stewart (Greece), Fred Warrick (Czech Republic), Allen Watson (Austria)
• Loyola College: Rod Platt (Austria), Jason Rowe (France)
• Maryland: Obinna Ekezie (Italy), Rodney Elliott (Turkey), John Gilchrist (Israel), Exree Hipp (Australia), Mike Mardesich (France), Drew Nicholas (Italy)
• UMBC: Serge Feckoua (France), Pascal Fleury (Canada)
• Morgan State: Tom Frederick (England)
• Navy: Sitapha Savane (Spain)
• Towson University: Ralph Biggs (Belgium), Matt Campbell (Australia), Tamir Goodman (Israel), Donald Jones (Argentina), Ryan Lexer (Israel), Dwayne Martin (England), Florian Schneider (France), Marijan Spalevic (Serbia)
Source: www.eurobasket.com.

*Update: Platt ended his career playing in Cyprus during the 2011-12 season. Andrew Kostecka, who ended his Loyola career in 2020, was playing this season for a team in Spain.*

# From the (Missouri) Valley to the Alps

*This story originally ran on the website of the Missouri Valley Conference in 2015 and is reprinted by permission.*

Ben Kandlbinder grew up in Washington, Mo., so he was well aware of the allure of the annual Valley basketball tournament, which has been held in St. Louis every year since 1991.
As a junior and senior at Missouri State he got to experience the championship game on a personal level as his school advanced to the title contest in 1997 and 1998 against Illinois State.
"They had a heck of a team. They were senior laden and it was back and forth the last couple of minutes," he recalls of the 1998 contest. "It was a great game and we knew we had to win to go to the NCAA Tournament."
But No.1 seed Illinois State prevailed both years, winning 84-74 in 1998 after beating No. 3 Missouri State by three points the previous season in the finale.
Kandlbinder was an all-tournament selection in 1998 and is among a slew of all-tourney picks from nearly three decades worth of Arch Madness that looks back fondly on those memories. A few years ago he took two of his three sons to the event as spectators as they made the drive of about 55 miles east to St. Louis.
"I loved coming back up for the tournament as a player. They always had good

crowds," notes Kandlbinder, now the Vice President/Owner of Aberi Steel in his hometown. "It was like a home away from home and a lot of my family got to come to see us play."

Other all-tournament performers who have made the transition to the business world includes Nate Green (Indiana State), an all-tourney player in 2000 who is now a Broker, Employee Benefits with Old National Insurance in Terre Haute, Ind.

"Playing in the tourney while in college was one of my fondest memories," Green reflects. "I think it is arguably one of the best tournaments in the country."

He played pro basketball in Austria for one year, in the D-League and then for several years in Italy through the 2009-10 season before moving back to The States.

"You are in a different country and seeing new sites and new people," Green recalls of his time overseas. "I was in Europe for the first time and seeing a melting pot of different cultures. It is kind of humbling to think about."

But he also knew when it was time to hang up the sneakers.

"When I decided not to play anymore my daughter, who is now 9, at the time she was a toddler. I had missed enough Christmases. I felt like it was time to hang it up. I was comfortable with the decision," he says.

Former Drake guard Adam Emmenecker was the Most Outstanding Player of the 2008 tourney as he led his team to a title game win against Illinois State by 30 points. He now works for the Principal Financial Group in Des Moines, Iowa, as a Business Operations Analyst.

"The first thing you remember is your teammates and the fun you had with those guys," he says. "It is fun to remember what happened in those games."

After graduating with a degree in business in 2008 he played one season of pro hoops in Frankfurt, Germany. "I had never been to Europe. You really don't know what to expect," he said.

Emmenecker, who is from Michigan, then played briefly in the D-league and about five years ago joined Principal Financial. "It is always difficult (to retire) because you are talking about a big lifestyle change," he notes. "To have the opportunity to play overseas was certainly fantastic."

## Still in the Game as Coaches

Several former Valley standouts have made the move to the real world but have been able to stay involved with basketball.

• Mark Morse, an all-tourney player for Tulsa in 1992, is now a coach and athletic director at Globe Institute of Technology, a technical college in New York City. Alvin "Pooh" Williamson (1995, Tulsa) is an assistant coach at Texas Tech under Tubby Smith, and Shea Seals, the MOP for Tulsa in 1996, is on the coaching staff at his alma mater after a playing career in the NBA, Europe and Asia.

• Chris Carr (Southern Illinois), an all-tourney player in 1994 and the MOP the following year as SIU won three straight titles from 1993-95.

What are his best memories of Arch Madness?

"Just being part of history, not only for my school by the Valley. We were the first team to win back-to-back-to-back titles. Being able to play that ESPN game on

Monday night with just two teams left and people watching, being a Missouri guy, was special," says Carr.

Carr spent several years in the NBA with Phoenix, Minnesota, New Jersey, Golden State, Chicago and Boston from 1995 to 2001 and also played in the former Yugoslavia and in Greece. He now lives in Eden Prairie, Minn., and is a coach with 43 Hoops Basketball Academy and at the prep level.

• Anthony Shavies (Missouri State) played in Austria and Ukraine and is now an instructor with the Missouri Basketball Academy.

"One of the best memories I have of the MVC tourney is back when we were getting ready to play Southern Illinois in the 2004 semifinals," according to Shavies. "I remember looking around during introductions and seeing the whole arena in maroon. Every fan was standing up and cheering as loud as they could and the game hadn't even started yet; the energy there was amazing. I get chills thinking about it."

Shavies joined the Missouri Basketball Academy less than a year ago. "It's been really satisfying to be able to share my knowledge of the game with the next generation of ball players out of southwest Missouri," he notes. "I run MBA along with fellow Bear alum Adam Leonard and another really good guy, Donn Gray, who grew up playing basketball with Adam."

### Still Active as Players

• Doug McDermott was a standout for Creighton but he was a small boy when he attended his first Valley tourney since his father was a coach at Northern Iowa before coaching his son.

The younger McDermott remembers walking on the concourse and paying $5 to play a free throw shooting contest at the tourney. "I probably spent all of my mother's purse money," McDermott, now with the Chicago Bulls, said in a telephone interview in late January.

"It is such a great environment," he says of Arch Madness. "The fans are into it."

He was an All-American at Creighton and scored 3,150 points. Now he is a rookie in the NBA and has had to work back from an injury. He had played in 18 games and was cleared to return to action in late January after he had knee surgery in mid-December.

"Having an injury during your rookie year isn't good," he said. "It is rough being a rookie in the NBA. It is a grind."

While The Valley has several players in the NBA, dozens more have kept their hoop careers alive by going overseas, notably to Europe.

• One of them is Randal Falker (Southern Illinois), who was the MOP of the 2006 tournament as SIU beat Bradley in the title game.

While he was not a big basketball fan as a boy, Falker was certainly aware of the Valley tourney since he went to Gateway Tech in St. Louis.

"Winning it for sure and being in the (NCAA) playoffs," said Falker, when asked for his best memories of the St. Louis event. "That was pretty awesome. It is not easy to win three games in a row."

Since college Falker has played in Turkey and is now in his sixth year in France, where he has learned some of the native language.

"I picked up a little. It is a very difficult language," he said in a telephone interview in late January from Nancy, France, which is about 90 minutes east of Paris. "I can get by; I can have a conversation in French."

Falker, like most American players in Europe, is provided the free use of an apartment and car and has very few expenses to go with his salary. He spends some of his free time cooking, one of his big hobbies.

On the court he has adapted to the European style of play, as some of the top leagues are in the western European countries of Spain, Italy and France. "I think France is more an NBA style league. It is an up and down league. You have a lot of (former) NBA players in France," said Falker.

• Booker Woodfox (Creighton), an all-tourney player in 2009, has been playing this season for the Texas Legends in the NBA D-League after earlier stops in China, Lebanon, Lithuania, Venezuela and Colombia. His best memory of the Valley tourney was the game-winning shot he hit as a senior versus Wichita State.

"That kind of put me on the map," Woodfox, who grew up near Dallas, said as his No. 2 seed team beat the Shockers, 63-62.

He has had two stints in Venezuela, which he calls his favorite country to play in. "I always felt I would be able to play somewhere. I didn't know where it would be," said Woodfox, who was averaging 10.3 points per game in late January for the Legends as a key reserve off the bench.

• Former Valley players who have been in the NBA this season include McDermott (Creighton, Chicago), Cleanthony Early (Wichita State, New York), Kyle Korver (Creighton, Atlanta) and Anthony Tolliver (Creighton), traded by Phoenix to Detroit in late December.

Korver, whose last Valley tourney was 2003, started the first 45 games this season for the Hawks and was averaging 13 points per contest.

"I loved playing in St. Louis every year," he said. "We won it three times. Every time you win that tournament it is a great feeling. My senior year we beat Southern Illinois. That was one of my favorite memories."

*Update: Korver last played in the NBA for the Bucks during the 2019-20 season. He scored nearly 12,000 regular-season points in the league.*

# JMU's Curry Was in Hoop-Crazy Country

*This story originally ran on the athletic website of JMU in 2019 and is reprinted with permission.*

Former James Madison standout Ron Curry had never been out of the country and now his plane was about to land in Europe, as his pro basketball career was ready to begin in Slovenia nearly three years ago. "It was surreal. I just got my passport the week before. It all happened so fast," recalls Curry, who played for the Dukes for four seasons through 2016.

Curry, 25, played last season in Germany and is winding down his third year as a pro hoopster in Europe, a typical destination for former Division I standouts who don't latch on with a team in the NBA or the G League. This season, he has been playing for a team in western Hungary.

"It is a good opportunity to play over here," said Curry, taking off his headphones to chat before a recent game here in the Hungarian Cup. "The biggest adjustment is the lifestyle. Basketball is the easy part, especially if you have good teammates. The hardest part is definitely adjusting to the European way of life, especially if you are not a big city in Germany - like a small town in Slovenia."

The small town to which he speaks is Novo Mesto, with about 23,000 people in southeastern Slovenia. He spent the 2017-18 season in metropolitan Bonn, Germany, then moved to Szombathely, a city of nearly 77,000 in western Hungary near the border with Slovenia.

The native of New Jersey is one of several former Dukes, both men and women, who have continued their careers overseas. Other former JMU hoopsters who played at the pro level during the 2018-19 season include Jackson Kent, a 2017 graduate of JMU with a degree in sport and recreation management.

Kent, about 250 miles northwest of Hungary, is playing in Nürnberg, Germany, known in America as Nuremberg. The city of about 500,000 in the southeast part of the country was the site of the Nürnberg trials for Nazis after World War II.

"I did know a little about the Nürnberg trials and have read up on it more after arriving," according to Kent, who played last season in the Czech Republic.

So, what are things like in Germany?

"A normal day for me is waking up for weight lifting three times a week and then practice during the evening. On days off, I walk around the city and try to see new places," according to Kent.

Another former JMU standout who played in Germany was Devon Moore, who was there during the 2017-18 season. He began his pro career in Hungary in 2013.

Closer to home, former JMU post presence Yohanny Dalembert, who played for the Dukes in 2016-17, was in a pro league in Canada this winter. He was averaging 3.5 points and 5.4 boards per contest in late February for Sudbury in the NBL-Canada.

A.J. Davis was the CAA Tournament Most Outstanding Player in 2013 when the Dukes last won the title and qualified for the NCAA field. Since then, Davis has played for pay in Canada, Mexico and made a stop in the G League.

Virginia Beach native Denzel Bowles, who ended his Dukes career in 2011, has had a long career overseas with stints in Lithuania, the Philippines, China, Venezuela, the United Arab Emirates, Lebanon, Puerto Rico, Israel and the Dominican Republic. The 6-foot-10 forward has played this season for Kanazawa in Japan, where he had 44 points in a game in December and was averaging 21 points and 11.3 rebounds per contest across his first 37 games.

Joey McLean has been playing in Dubai, according to Kent, his former high school teammate, while Andrey Semenov has been playing in his native Russia

Former JMU women who have played in pro leagues this winter include WNBA draft picks Tamera Young (Israel) and Jazmon Gwathmey (Spain), as well as Jasmine Gill (Czech Republic) and Precious Hall (Sweden). Local product Kirby Burkholder of Turner Ashby High played in Hungary from 2016-18 after being named CAA Player of the Year in 2014.

Curry was part of the JMU title team as a freshman in 2013, then gained All-CAA honors in 2015 and 2016, when he averaged 17.2 points per contest.

The 6-foot-3 guard was part of the regular-season champions in Slovenia in 2017 and was named to the All-Import Team, according to EuroBasket.com, as he averaged 12 points per contest in league games and more than 11 per game in 26 Adriatic League games.

Curry had nine points on Feb. 16 as his team lost in the Hungarian Cup finals to a team that include American guard Andrew Rowsey, from Lexington, Va. Curry was averaging 14.7 points per contest in Hungarian league games.

Hungary is about the size of Indiana, but only has about 10 million residents with nearly 20 percent of those living in capital Budapest. Hungary was under Communist rule until the late 1980s, around the time the Berlin Wall came down. The Hungarian language is among the hardest for non-native speakers to learn, with 14 vowels just for starters.

But English is the common language for most of the pro basketball leagues in Europe and that is no exception for Curry. His coach this season is Gasper Okorn, who speaks English and is from bordering Slovenia. "I was aware of him, since he played in Slovenia," Okorn said.

Curry said it takes an open mind to adjust to new cultures overseas.

"I didn't know this would be my path. The places I have been to, it has been good to see different cultures and things you don't see in America," Curry said.

*Update: Curry began the 2021-22 season playing for a team in Riga, Latvia. Davis, who played in Mexico and in the minors in North America, was injured in 2021 when he was hit by a car in Ohio and his former JMU teammates have rallied to support him. Davis and Moore attended a JMU home game early in the 2021-22 season. Several former JMU players took part in The Basketball Tournament in the United State in 2021, and Davis was on hand to watch. Moore played in Germany during the 2020-21 season after earlier stops in Hungary, Ukraine and Germany. He was part of the JMU team that took part in the NCAA tournament in 2013 after winning the CAA title. In the fall of 2021, JMU announced it was moving to the Sun Belt Conference.*

# Western Illinois Grad Felt at Home

*This story originally ran on the website of Western Illinois in 2016 and was reprinted with permission.*

In the second installment of a three-part series leading into The Summit League Basketball Championships, we take a look at another former student-athlete now playing pro basketball overseas. David Driver, a writer who has covered overseas basketball for more than 10 years, touched base with former Western Illinois standout Ceola Clark III.

Clark is a 6-foot-3 guard who was The Summit Defensive Player of the Year in 2010 and 2012 and an all-league performer during his career. In 2013, he helped Western Illinois win a share of the regular-season title when he scored 12.5 points per contest.

DD: What city are you living in now and how would you describe the city, and what people do for a living and entertainment?

Clark: I am currently living in Sentjur, Slovenia. It is a very small city but the people here enjoy their basketball. The city reminds me a lot of Macomb, Ill., where I played college basketball, in the sense of it being a small town and people in the area are really pulling for a successful basketball club. There isn't much entertainment here but I would have to say basketball is after coming off a national championship last season that I was blessed to be a part of.

DD: What is your living situation like - does the club provide a free apartment and a car?

Clark: I currently stay in a three-bedroom flat that me and another American on the team share. Since the city isn't that big a car is not needed. Everything here is pretty much walking distance but I find myself taking the train often when going to other neighboring cities.

DD: What do you do with your free time?

Clark: In my free time, I watch a lot of movies, TV shows, NBA and NCAAM basketball games. I would also consider myself a "Game Head". I play a lot of games on my PS4 (Call of Duty, Madden, NBA2K16, FIFA16, Grand Theft Auto). When I do get a chance to go out a few of my teammates and myself go bowling, go-kart riding and occasionally play some pool.

DD: How would you compare the level of play in your current league with that of The Summit League?

Clark: The level here is much tougher than playing in The Summit League. I am not taking anything away from The Summit but being a professional takes a lot of hard work and dedication. There are many former NBA players in this league as we play in the Euro League, the highest league in Europe.

DD: How did college prepare you for where you are now?

Clark: I think playing at Western Illinois under Jim Molinari and current head coach Billy Wright helped me out tremendously. We ran a ball screen type offense under Molinari which allowed the basketball to be in my hands and helped me read situations. This is very similar to the game here in Europe. Coach Wright helped me along the way also during film sessions and many talks throughout the season. He was a former player that played point guard and took his team very far and I tried to pick his brain as much as possible. He is still someone I can call or email with anything I have questions about. I am thankful today for everyone that coached me at Western Illinois because they were, and still are, a big key to my success.

DD: When did you start playing with your current team?

Clark: This is my second year in Sentjur, Slovenia as I played last season and currently am playing for the same club again (Tajfun).

DD: What are the biggest challenges you face on and off the court at this time? How many total Americans are on the team now?

Clark: Some of the biggest challenges I face on and off the court are not playing and being around my family. These past two years have been a little rough for me not playing and being around my family but I know being a professional basketball player is something I've always dreamed about. There are currently two Americans on this team.

DD: What was your major in college and what year did you graduate?
Clark: I left Western Illinois in 2013 as a finance major with a minor in marketing.

DD: What have you learned about overseas basketball that you did not realize before you came?
Clark: I can probably say the one thing that I've learned about basketball overseas that I didn't realize before I came is how talented many of the players are here and at such a young age. The basketball IQ is very high in terms of reading situations. I think having a 24 second shot clock overseas at such a young age makes players learn the game faster and puts them in situations to make decisions more often.

DD: What have been some of your memorable moments overseas?
Clark: I would say my entire season last year was one of the greatest times of my basketball career. First, winning the three-point competition as well as hitting the game-winning shot in the All Star game. Second, being a part of an historical season in which we won the Slovenian National Championship for the first time in club history.

*Update: Clark retired in 2016. James Claar, who ended his career at Western Illinois in 2020, has played the past two seasons for the Belfast Star in Ireland.*

# Dayton, Lehigh Stars Part of Same Prep Power

*This story originally ran on patch.com in Maryland in 2011 and was reprinted by permission.*

David Morris, a former basketball standout at St. Vincent Pallotti High in Laurel, graduated from the University of Dayton with a degree in communications. But his education continued in a new way after those years in Ohio.

A former starting point guard at the Division I level, Morris played pro hoops in Germany, Romania and Spain after a four-year career at Dayton.

One of those learning experiences came a few years ago when he was playing for a pro team in Romania, a country in eastern Europe where life for many is very difficult.

His team, which included some Serbian players, made a trip to Belgrade to play a Euro Cup game. While in Serbia's capital, Morris saw the buildings bombed from NATO air strikes in the late 1990s.

"It still affected a lot of Serbians, even now, which I didn't know. My teammates were pretty mad about the situation. I had no idea it affected Serbians like that," said Morris, who grew up in Hyattsville.

As a point guard for Pallotti in the late 1990s he led the Panthers to the title game of the Washington Catholic Athletic Conference (WCAC) tournament as a senior.

The Panthers fell in the closing seconds to Hyattsville powerhouse DeMatha, which had two future NBA players (Joe Forte and Keith Bogans) on its team.

While Forte and Bogans went to the NBA, Morris was one of several players from that Pallotti team to play overseas. The list includes Nate Green (University of Dayton); Kenny Whitehead (Charlotte, James Madison); and Austen Rowland, (Delaware and Lehigh).

This year's NBA draft, held June 23, again included several players chosen from Europe.

Rowland has played in Austria and Germany, and spent this season in France. "It is not a problem for me," he told Patch on Thursday of spending most of the year away from family and friends. "I have learned how to do it. My first few years it was a challenge."

A point guard from Hyattsville, Rowland spends his summers at his home in Florida. He is slated to play for a new team in France next season and will head back to Europe in August.

"Being a professional and getting along with players from other countries" can be difficult, Rowland said. "I try to learn things about other countries. Be humble and realize the United States is not the only country in the world."

Basketball has even taken Rowland to China, where he played in exhibition games while with a team from Germany. He has also been to London, Amsterdam, Belgium, Lithuania, Latvia, Estonia and Luxembourg. Rowland was once in the same league in Germany with Whitehead, but they did not play against each other.

Rowland, who turns 30 this summer, said he hopes to play overseas four or five more years.

Another Pallotti product, Keith Lambkin, ended his college career at Canisius in 1999 and played pro ball in Germany and this season in Luxembourg.

Green played in Austria and Luxembourg in 2003-04, in his first year out of college, and later played in Mexico, Ecuador and most recently Argentina during the 2008-09 season, according to eurobasket.com.

Morris, 30, who now lives in the Beltsville area, ended his pro career about two years ago. He has remained close to Rowland, a guard who last month finished the pro hoop season with a team in France by averaging 13.1 points per game for Le Portel.

Rowland was the Patriot League player of the year in his only season at Lehigh. He played his first three years of college at Delaware.

Morris was a point guard at Dayton and help the Flyers make the NCAA tournament during his career. He and Green, a forward, were teammates at both Pallotti and Dayton.

Whitehead, a center, ended his career at JMU in 2003 and went on to play in Germany, Cyprus, Switzerland, Turkey, Israel and France, according to eurobasket.com

While overseas, Morris visited Eiffel Tower in Paris, the site of the Berlin Wall in Germany and the Charles Bridge in Prague. He was also able to visit Hungary, Belgium and Amsterdam.

"Germany is like my second home. Austen and I know lot of people there," Morris said.

So what were the highlights of playing in Europe? "Just the culture, getting to understand a new, different culture outside of the United States was great actually," Morris said. "Things were a lot more open there."

One drawback of playing overseas was when Morris did not get paid on time by his club. This is common among American players in some European countries. "That factored into my decision" to return to the U.S., Morris said.

On the other hand, American players in top leagues in Europe are normally given the free use of an apartment, a car and vouchers for food. Most American players get a tax-free salary and can make close to $100,000 per season in some of the western European leagues. Leagues in Romania, Hungary and eastern Europe usually have fewer resources for American college products.

"There are very few expenses," Morris said.

While in college, Morris went with Dayton for an overseas trip to Australia and that was just the beginning of his hoop travels.

Today, Morris works at as an account executive at Stone Street Capital, a structure settlement company in Bethesda. "Basketball helped me out a lot. I studied marketing at Dayton, even though my degree is in communications," he said.

And he got another education once he headed to Europe.

*Update: Morris ended his career in Romania in 2009 while Rowland played in France in 2018-19 after working as an assistant coach at Lehigh. Josh Cunningham, who ended his career at Dayton in 2019, was with a team in Bosnia this season. Ex-Lehigh star Austin Price began this season with a team in The Netherlands.*

# Norfolk State, Kansas Products Team Up

*This story originally appeared in the Daily Press in 2005 and was reprinted with permission.*

Prague — Former William and Mary player Adam Hess finds a professional career in the Czech Republic. Adam Hess joined a veteran team for his first season of professional basketball, albeit far from his College of William and Mary roots.

His teammates with Nymburk in the Czech Republic include former Norfolk State standout Maurice Whitfield, and ex-University of Kansas player Ashante Johnson.

"He came into a good situation. He doesn't have to be the go-to guy," Whitfield said of Hess, who averaged more than 20 points per game his last two college seasons in Williamsburg. "We didn't need him to come in and score 30 points every game."

But in one magical game, just a few days before Christmas, Hess did even better than that, setting a Czech record in the National Basketball League with a 55-point explosion in a road victory.

It was the most points Hess has ever scored in a game, at any level. He made eight of 15 shots from 3-point range, three of four free throws and 14 two-point field goals.

"I fired up some shots," admitted the 6-foot-7 Hess, sitting in a dark auxiliary gymnasium before a road game here in March.

There was a reason for his greediness that day. Most European leagues, including the Czech Republic, allow only two non-Europeans (almost always Americans) per team. Johnson had recently rejoined the team after a short absence for personal reasons, and the team's coaches planned to use Whitfield and Johnson as its American players for several games. Hess was about to become a full-time bench-warmer. So he asked if he could play the whole game.

"It was my last game for awhile. You might as well play the whole game," Hess said.

The move paid off.

Whitfield became a Czech citizen a few days later, leaving Hess and Johnson as the team's two non-European players.

Hess is averaging 14.6 points and 21.7 minutes per game. He was selected to play in the Czech all-star game that will be held Monday. He was also invited to take part in the 3-point shootout. Whitfield will play for the Czech team in the exhibition, while Johnson will join Hess on the import roster.

Hess' European adventure began with help from Terry Driscoll, William and Mary's athletic director. Driscoll, who played at Boston College and in Italy, hooked Hess up with general manager at Fabriano, a team in Italy's B League that features former University of Virginia player Jamal Robinson. Hess played a few weeks in Italy before the team released him.

"They wanted more of a slasher guy. I was more of a shooter," he said.

After heading home to Michigan, Hess was contacted by Nymburk and signed a two-year deal. His father, Doug, played basketball at the University of Toledo. Doug graduated in 1971, and after being cut by Kentucky of the old NBA he played briefly in Italy, Belgium and the CBA. He saw his son play several times last fall.

"The European players are much better now. It is much better," Doug Hess said recently from his home in Michigan. The elder Hess saw his son play several games last fall in the Czech Republic.

Hess' team is 26-1 in Czech league games and 37-8 overall going into a home game today with the same Sparta Prague team that Nymburk easily beat earlier this month.

Like most top American players in Europe, Hess is provided the free use of an apartment and a new car by his team. He gets several free meals per week and a tax-free salary.

"I thought it would be a huge difference from living at home, but there aren't as many differences as I thought," Hess said. To ease the transition, his parents have visited him several times.

Hess has been to Germany, Poland, Belgium, Israel, Bulgaria and Russia for road games this season. "St. Petersburg (in Russia) was really neat. I don't have a good (sense of) Russian history," said Hess, an Academic All-American at William and Mary with a degree in finance.

Hess is the second player in as many seasons to earn All-CAA honors and then head to the Czech League. Craig Callahan, part of NCAA tournament teams at UNC Wilmington, is one of the top scorers and rebounders in his second season in the Czech Republic.

Hess said it is just a coincidence that he followed Callahan to the Czech Republic, which until a 1989 revolution was part of the Communist bloc. The country split off from what is now Slovakia in 1993. Hess played mostly power forward his last two seasons in college. Now he plays shooting guard and small forward.

"The biggest adjustment is not playing (nearly) 40 minutes per game," he said.

Which helped to make his rookie debut a little easier.

"He is a great guy, on and off the court," said Whitfield, the former Norfolk State star.

*Update: Hess ended his overseas career in Germany in 2016. Former Norfolk State standout Pendarvis Williams, a guard from Philadelphia, was with a team in northern Italy this season after earlier stops in Germany and France.*

# Oral Roberts Star Excelled

*This story originally ran on the athletic website of Oral Roberts in Oklahoma in 2016 and was reprinted by permission.*

In the third and final installment of a three-part series leading into The Summit League Basketball Championships, we take a look at another former student-athlete now playing pro basketball overseas. David Driver, a writer who has covered overseas basketball for more than 10 years, touched base with former Oral Roberts standout Dominique Allen.

Allen was born in England in 1989 and finished her college career at Oral Roberts playing 31 games during the 2011-12 season. She was part of ORU's regular-season championship squads in 2010 and 2011, advancing to The Summit League Championship Game in 2010.

Allen averaged nearly 11 points and eight rebounds per game in her first pro season, 2012-13 in Italy. She then played in France in 2013-14, and averaged 6.8 points and 5.4 rebounds per contest.

Allen spent the 2014-15 season with a team in the Czech Republic and averaged 6.0 points and 5.1 rebounds per contest. She began the 2015-16 season with a team in Austria and then moved to a league in Germany. She had eight points for Chemnitz in a game in mid-January and one of her teammates was a fellow-Summit League alumnae, Brooke LeMar, a Californian who finished her college career with North Dakota State in 2015.

DD: Where are you playing now and what is the city like?
Allen: I am currently living in Chemnitz, Germany. I only recently arrived at this club so I haven't had the time to really have a look around the city. So far everyone has been extremely nice and welcoming. The club provides a fully-furnished

apartment and a team car. We live very close to the city center and our gym, so everything is in walking distance. In my free time I like to explore the city, do some sightseeing and get to know the culture of the city I'm living in. I love exploring new places and experiencing a new culture.

DD: When did you finish up at Oral Roberts?
Allen: I graduated four years ago and I've played professionally in five different countries since then and each country is very different. The Summit League prepared me extremely well for playing professionally in Europe. The intensity of practices and games definitely helped me transition from college athlete to a professional.

DD: Where did you grow up and where have you played pro ball?
Allen: I'm English and I played in England until I was 18 and left to attend Oral Roberts University. Since 2012, I have played in Bologna, Italy; Calais, France; Ostrava, Czech Republic; Vienna, Austria and Chemnitz, Germany.

DD: What are the biggest challenges that you face playing overseas?
Allen: The only challenges I find off the court is finding something to do with my spare time. On the court can be hard if there is a language barrier, and getting used to the style of play in that country. There are three Americans on the team and our coach is also American.

DD: What has it been like to play pro basketball away from your native country?
Allen: The most amazing thing about playing overseas is how many different people from different countries you get to meet. I love how much I get to travel and see places that I would never have the chance to see if it wasn't for basketball. One of my favorite memories was when I got to take my mum to Florence and Milan while I was playing in Italy. My favorite city that I have played in was Vienna. Vienna is the most beautiful city with so many things to do.

   *Update: Allen began the 2021-22 season playing for Manchester in the British League.*

# Life After the WNBA

   *This story originally ran in the Stafford County Sun in Virginia in 2014 and was reprinted by permission.*

Chay Shegog, 24, after a standout career at the University of North Carolina, headed overseas to play pro basketball after she was waived by the Connecticut Sun of the WNBA in 2012.

The Brooke Point High School graduate first played in Hungary and since then she has also played with teams based in France, Australia and now China.

"The biggest adjustment on the court is the style of play," she wrote in e-mail in December. "Each country is different and they have different principles than teams that I've played for in the states. When I say principles I mean things in regards to help side defense, and how players rotate. It was difficult to adjust at first, but once you get the hang of it, it's not that bad."

"And the biggest adjustment off the court with anywhere I go overseas deals with food," she added. "I don't eat meat, and every dish here in China is made with meat so I've really been living off of eggs, noodles, and rice for the past two months. Sometimes when we go to different cities, I can get Subway or Pizza Hut, but that's only if I'm lucky."

Americans overseas have to adjust to how and spend their free time, since they no longer have to take classes when playing at the Division I level in college.

"Life in China is pretty busy," notes Shegog, drafted 21st overall by Connecticut out of North Carolina. "I live on a sports campus and they have us on a really tight schedule. We wake up for breakfast at 7, train at 9, have lunch at 11, and then have a little bit of downtime in the afternoon before practice around 3. Then we fill the rest of the day with meetings and film sessions so down time is pretty rare."

"But the team provides me with everything I need to live comfortably overseas. I actually haven't had a chance to explore the city that I live in or really any other city we visit, everything is strictly basketball," adds the center.

While playing Hungary, which has a strong women's league, her team took part in domestic games and also played in the EuroLeague. That meant games in other countries; basketball has taken Shegog to Spain, Austria, Germany, Russia, the Czech Republic, Poland, Finland and Romania.

Shegog says each team in China is allowed one import player. That is different than many men's leagues in Europe, where countries such as Hungary allow three foreign players per team while in Germany the men's league has a roster filled with mostly Americans.

But the opportunities for American women overseas in basketball are fewer than their male counterparts.

"In China, there's only one import on each team. And the level of competition is fierce. Usually the Americans they sign are WNBA All-Stars or U.S. Olympians," Shegog notes. "My first game was actually against my favorite player as a kid - Sylvia Fowles. It kind of gave me a taste of how guys in the NBA felt when they finally made it to the league and had to go against Kobe (Bryant) or Lebron (James). But players like Fowles, Brittney Griner, Maya Moore, and Candace Dupree play out here and its overall been a really good experience to play against such talent."

Shegog was a Parade All-American at Brooke Point and she scored more than 1,600 points there. While at UNC she scored more than 1,000 points and was among the top players in the Atlantic Coast Conference.

Her brother, Anthony, has played this season for the football team at Virginia Tech. The Hokies play Cincinnati on Dec. 27 in the Military Bowl in Annapolis, Maryland.

*Update: Shegog later played in Poland and last played overseas in Romania in 2017. She returned to teach and coach high school basketball in Stafford, Virginia. "We love being around basketball and teaching the kids. And making it work," she told the Free-Lance Star of Fredericksburg in 2021 of her coaching staff.*

# Have Hoops, Will Travel

*This story originally appeared in the alumni magazine of the University of Cincinnati in 2012 and was reprinted by permission.*

While many UC hoopsters began their college careers with an eye on playing professionally, the law of supply and demand often hit home. Although the NBA and WNBA have drafted plenty of Bearcats, dozens of former UC ballers have carved out a nice career, as well as a profitable one, by playing hoops around the globe.

Take Tony Bobbitt, for instance. After finishing his UC career in '04, he saw his NBA dreams come to a halt a year later when he was waived by the perennial title-contender Los Angeles Lakers.

Bearcat fans may best remember Bobbitt for two big shots -- the game-winner he sunk his senior year in the final seconds of the opening NCAA tourney round against East Tennessee State and the painful low blow he sustained a week earlier when DePaul's LeVar Seals punched him in the groin. Bobbitt eventually got up off the hardwood and finished the game with 17 points to help UC to yet another Conference USA championship.

Such determination kept Bobbitt from letting the Lakers end his pro career. Instead, it launched a global sojourn of playing in Italy, Germany, Cyprus and Mexico. These days, heÕs back in the states in the NBA Development League with the Idaho Stampede.

"The advantages you have overseas are being provided with a free car, a free place to stay and making good money," Bobbitt says. "The fans over there are really, really into basketball."

Cincinnati native Michelle Jones recalls fans coming out to watch her first practice in Finland at the beginning of the '10-11 season. "They just wanted to see who the new American player was. People take it seriously over there. The whole town was at our first game."

Her team was more popular than the local men's team and drew more fans than some of her college games, notes Jones, after returning to Cincinnati to be with her 4-year-old son who had stayed with family members while she was abroad

At last check, 14 men and two women who once wore the C-Paw are playing overseas, including Kareem Johnson, who began this season in Switzerland after stops in Spain, New Zealand and Slovakia. Immanuel McElroy has been playing in Germany since '04, and Cedric McGowan, who began this season in Argentina, has also seen time in Finland, the Netherlands, Uruguay and Mexico.

Pete Mickeal has played in Greece, Russia and South Korea and began the '11-12 campaign in Spain, which has one of the top leagues in Europe. Rashad Bishop began this season in Israel before heading to Brazil. Adam Hrycaniuk was in his native Poland. Steve Toyloy played in Turkey last season, and Nick Williams, one of the few Americans to play in Bosnia since the Balkan Wars of the 1990s, began this season in Germany before heading to Hungary.

Even UC players with significant NBA experience have stamped their passports in foreign lands. DerMarr Johnson has played in Italy, Puerto Rico and China. Kenyon Martin played in China in 2011 before returning to the NBA with the LA Clippers. James White is in Italy after playing

## Not always a vacation

Playing overseas is not just fun and games. While most top Americans with Division I experience can expect free housing and the use of a car from European clubs, there are drawbacks. Not only do players find themselves in a culture in which everyone does not speak English, but their teammates may only include one or two other Americans.

"You have to be self-reliant and tough -- mentally and physically," says associate head coach Larry Davis, who has made recruiting trips to Europe. "You are isolated, especially when you first get there."

Madinah Slaise, one of the top scorers in UC women's history, recalls those early days in France, Switzerland and Israel, following her one WNBA season in Detroit in 2000. "I was 22 years old, living in another country and couldn't just pick up the phone and call my mother.

"In Switzerland, I was the only English-speaking player, and the coach would speak in his native language," says Slaise, now stationed overseas in the U.S. Air Force. "Everyone knew that I was getting paid more than the (local) players who were there. It was a lot to handle for a kid just out of college."

Today, American men in lower-level European leagues can start out around $50,000 per season while NBA-caliber players in western Europe or Russia can pull in high six figures. But American players, men and women, are almost always expected to be the top scorers for their teams.

"The general manager may threaten to fire you if you don't get enough rebounds," says coach

The biggest adjustment overseas, according to '09 grad Mike Williams, was getting used to the rules used by FIBA, the governing body of international basketball. Some of the rules differ from those at the NCAA Division I level and the NBA level. For instance, under FIBA rules, touching the ball in the cylinder is not goaltending, and a player has to clearly dribble the ball first before picking up his pivot foot.

Williams says his pro career in Zwolle, The Netherlands, was his first time out of the United States. "I was always open to going to a different country because it is the sport I love. I don't care what country I'm playing in. For me, it was not really an adjustment. Everything just worked out. I don't get homesick because I like to travel and see new things."

Since '06-07, when Mick Cronin, A&S '97, became UC men's head coach, the Bearcats have sent seven players overseas. The coach and his staff assist players who want to play pro ball overseas.

Coach Davis recalls Deonta Vaughn, who averaged 11.7 points and 3.5 assists his senior year in 2010. When the NBA failed to pan out, his agent focused on options abroad. "We talked to him about how to succeed over there," Davis says. As a rookie pro in Poland in '10-11, the 6-foot-1 guard nearly duplicated his senior-year stats by averaging 11.6 points and 3.5 assists. This year, he is lacing up his sneakers in Ukraine.

Kristen "K.B." Sharp has played pro ball ever since ending her Bearcat career in '03. First, she spent time in the WNBA with New York, Indiana and Chicago, then signed a two-year contract with USO Mondeville in France in '10. Last season, she was a second-team All-French player. This season, she averaged 11 points and four assists in her first 10 games.

"In Normandy, life is simpler," she says. "It is smaller than America. It is a historic town where World War II happened. There are remains of castles. Of course, it is a job. But for me, it is a pleasure. It is still fun for me to play. I really fell in love with France. I speak French fluently, and I am trying to become a French citizen. I like the country. I like the life here. I love the food. Maybe I will live here after my career is over."

*Update: Overseas veteran Stephenson played in China during the 2019-20 season.*

# Photo Gallery

**VITTO BROWN**

*Brown, 26, was born in Oklahoma, went to high school in Ohio and was a four-year standout at the University of Wisconsin through 2017. He played in France before taking part in the Las Vegas summer league with the Phoenix Suns in 2021; he was averaging about 12 points per game in December for Real Betis, a team in Seville, Spain.*

Photo Courtesy of Real Betis

## TAYLOR KOENEN

*Koenen has played this season for Ferrol in western Spain. She ended her college career at UNC in 2020 and played in Switzerland in her first season as a rookie pro.*

Photo Courtesy of Baxi Ferrol basketball, Spain

## DANNY AGBELESE

*Agbelese played in college at Hampton in Virginia and began the 2021-22 pro season with Real Betis, in Seville, Spain. He has also played in Uruguay, Spain, Greece, and France.*

Photo by David Driver

## J.J. MANN

*Mann and his wife, Amy Jo, take a break at a holiday market in Brussels in 2016. Mann, a former Belmont basketball star, played in Austria and Germany and after Belgium played in Kosovo, Denmark, Portugal, and Germany. The Georgia native was with the Bayer Giants to begin the 2021-22 season and was averaging about 11 points per game. Mann was the player of the year in the Ohio Valley Conference and played in March Madness with Belmont.*

Photo by Liz Driver

## OMAR PREWITT

*Omar Prewitt played prep hoops in basketball-crazy Kentucky in Montgomery County, then was a four-year standout at William & Mary in Virginia. Since then he has played for pay in Lithuania, Greece, Poland (photo in Warsaw), Turkey, Czech Republic, and Germany. Prewitt began this season with Bamberg, in the Bavarian region of Germany.*

Photo by David Driver

## XAVIER THAMES

*Thames, 31, a native of Sacramento, California, played in college at Washington State and San Diego State and was drafted in the second round by Toronto in 2014. Since then, he has played in Seville, Spain, and with pro teams in Macedonia, Israel, Greece and New Zealand, as well as a minor league team in Fort Wayne, Indiana. As of December, he was averaging 13.1 points and 4.0 assists per contest for Debrecen in the northeast corner of Hungary. He played at Pleasant Grove High in Elk Grove, California.*

Courtesy Hungarian Basketball Federation

## KRISTI TOLIVER

*"Last year not playing, and just watching all of the things that were happening ... as a viewer watching the games I was extremely proud of the message that was being sent," veteran pro Kristi Toliver told the author in 2021 after sitting out the WNBA season in 2020 to focus in part on social justice issues. "The women in this league have always been leaders for the right things. I'm just extremely proud to be a part of that." Toliver was a standout at Harrisonburg High in Virginia and helped lead Maryland to the NCAA title in 2006 as a freshman guard. After college, she played several years overseas, including a long stint in Russia. Toliver aided Washington to the WNBA title in 2019 before signing with Los Angeles. Her father, George, is a former referee in the NBA. She signed in August 2021 to be an assistant coach with Dallas in the NBA after also being on the staff of the Wizards.*

Photo Courtesy of Los Angeles Sparks

## LESLIE KNIGHT

*Knight, who played at the University of Minnesota, signs autographs for young fans after a game in October 2021 in Madrid, Spain. She began her pro career in Switzerland in 2008 and has played in Spain since 2009.*

Photo by David Driver

### RONALD CURRY
*Curry played at Paul VI High in New Jersey and ended his college career at JMU in Virginia in 2016. Since then he has played at the pro level in Slovenia, Germany, Hungary, and Latvia. The 6-foot-4 guard was with a team in Riga, Latvia to start the 2021-22 campaign.*

Photo Courtesy of Nemzeti Bajnokság I/A (Basketball Champions League) of Hungary

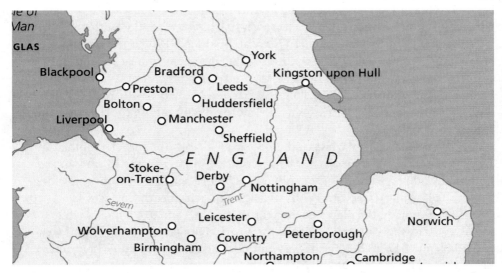

# WNBA Players Burn Candle at Both Ends

*This story appeared in globalsportsmatters.com in 2019.*

Christie Rogers knew at an early age she wanted to be a basketball coach. She played high school and Division III basketball in her native Maryland. Before joining the staff at Clemson University, she served as a coaches' intern for the Washington Mystics of the WNBA.

She assisted with individual workouts for players with the Mystics, helped scout opponents and to plan practice sessions. And she learned more than 10 years ago about a WNBA practice that has been going on for at least a decade: Many top WNBA players, including many Americans, are forced to juggle playing overseas in the winter with a WNBA career in the summer.

"They have to play both seasons," said Rogers, an assistant this season with Radford of the Big South Conference. "I worked for the Mystics in 2008, and our whole team played overseas. When training camp started in April and May, some of the players weren't even back yet."

Not only do American women have to play at a high level most of the year, those that head overseas deal with the challenges of risk of injury, a new culture and language.

In the past few years, high-profile players like Chiney Ogwumike and Breanna Stewart have been injured while playing this second season.

Unless an American heads to England, which doesn't have a high-level women's league, she is most likely dealing with a language other than English when she goes out to eat or make a run for coffee.

That is certainly the case for former University of Maryland standout Shatori Walker-Kimbrough, 22, who is playing this season in Miskolc, a city in the northern part of Hungary. The Hungarian language is considered one of the hardest for non-native speakers to learn - it has 14 vowels and 44 letters.

"Being that I don't watch much TV, except for some NBA games, I spend much of my time reading," said Walker-Kimbrough, who grew up near Pittsburgh. "The adjustment for me on and off the court is pretty much the same. For me, when I come to a new country, it's the language barrier. Many of my teammates speak English, so the language barrier is a little more difficult off the court – for example at the grocery store."

She played four years at Maryland. She was an all-Big Ten player, helping the Terps make the Final Four twice. She was drafted in 2017 by the Mystics as the sixth pick and played in Belgium and France before heading to Hungary, which has attracted Americans with WNBA backgrounds for nearly 15 years.

Kirby Burkholder, the player of the year in the CAA in 2014 while playing for James Madison University, played for ZTE in Hungary in 2016-17 and was in Miskolc in 2017-18 before she was injured. Earlier, she played in Italy and Belgium. "There is a language barrier with each team," according to Burkholder, who tried out for the Mystics before heading overseas. "For example, my coach in Italy didn't speak English."

Forward Reshanda Gray and guard Lexie Brown have played this season in Hungary for Gyor. Gray was drafted by Minnesota in the second round out of Cal and played in 30 games for the Atlanta Dream in 2016. For Gyor, she had 20 points in 20 minutes in a win March 16 and was averaging nearly 15 points per contest. Brown, drafted out of Duke by Connecticut, played in 22 games with the Sun last summer.

Another common destination for American women is Belgium. That is where former Rutgers star Kahleah Copper played during the 2016-17 season. The Philadelphia native averaged 7.1 points per game for Chicago in the WNBA in 2018 and has played this winter in Turkey.

"It was a big adjustment for me on and off the court," Copper said of being overseas. "Off the court: first, the streets are very different here, so driving was my first adjustment. There aren't many street signs and the person to the right has the priority. That's very important here because there aren't many stop signs, so I have to really pay attention. Also many of their stores close early so if I need groceries I have to shop early."

WNBA players head overseas, usually to Europe, to make money and play at a high level. Unlike their NBA counterparts, the WNBA season is much shorter and the pay much less.

On average, WNBA players make $71,635 in 2017 while the maximum salary was $115,500 for veterans who've been in the league for at least six years. The average for the 2018 season was in the $79,000 range.

According to Forbes, the average NBA salary is projected to reach $10 million for the 2020-21 season thanks to the new labor deal and the league's nine-year, $24 billion TV agreement with ESPN/TNT reached in 2014. The current average NBA salary of $6.2 million for the 2018-19 season is tops across all sports.

"It's because of the WNBA that we're able to make good money playing overseas in the first place and make a name for ourselves," former Duke standout Elizabeth Williams told The Guardian. "And there's a lot of things that go into playing basketball here that you don't think about, and you realize how much you miss when you're overseas. Being away from family and friends for an extended period of time is tough. It's a sacrifice."

Nearly 90 out of 144 players on WNBA rosters in 2018 spent time playing overseas during their offseason, The Guardian reported in 2018.

"In the WNBA, the maximum income a player could earn in 2016 was $109,000. In Russia, that number is tripled for one season, and, as of 2014, a player could earn an estimated $600,000 playing in China," according to The Undefeated.

Former Nebraska standout Jordan Hooper is playing this season for a team in Holon, Israel, and she played all 40 minutes March 21.

"I would love to stay in the states and play one season and one season only and have an offseason where I could get to work out really hard with some trainers and a nutritionist like LeBron (James does)," Hooper told The Guardian.

That doesn't appear likely to happen. So American women have to adjust overseas, as do some of their former NCAA male counterparts who are not good enough for the NBA and want to make more money in Europe than in minor leagues in North America.

Mackenzie Latt, a standout at Davidson through 2018, arrived in Portugal last fall for her first season of pro hoops. She was still dealing with jet lag as she took the court for her first exhibition game.

"I was like a fish out of water," said Latt, sitting in a coffee shop in Lisbon in January. "I was completely lost."

It is a feeling many of her fellow Americans with a WNBA pedigree experience in Europe.

*Update: Walker-Kimbrough played for Connecticut and Washington in the WNBA in 2021 and began the 2021-22 season overseas in Israel.*

# From Belmont to Brussels

*This story originally ran in the Tennessean in 2016 and is reprinted by permission.*

**B**russels — Former Belmont basketball star J.J. Mann sat in the Café Velvet one recent morning in Brussels, the bustling, diverse New York City-like capital of Belgium and home to the European Union.

The previous night in a game that began at the customary time of 8:30 p.m. local time — "a little bit past my bedtime," he joked — Mann was held to six points as his team lost 82-72 at home against a team from Germany about 45 minutes southwest of Brussels.

Now he and his wife, the former Amy Jo Anderson, a four-year soccer player at Belmont, made the drive to the capital for an interview and some sightseeing on a rare off day in a country that follows the European model of two practices per day for basketball during the week.

Mann, who ended his career at Belmont in 2014, is in his third season as a pro in Europe. He made previous stops in Austria and Germany; this year he is with Mons-Hainaut, which is allowed six foreign players on a 12-man roster.

After college, his pro career started with a 10-day stay with a team in Poland.

Mons was home to a convent in the seventh century and was once a fortified camp constructed by Roman legions, according to Frommer's guidebook.

"The city is great," said Mann, a 6-foot-6 shooting guard and small forward.

He was married in 2015 at Arrington Vineyards, south of Nashville, and his wife was with him last season in Germany.

"It is not go, go, go like it is in the States, which I enjoy," said Amy Jo, who is from Birmingham, Ala. "When you go out for a meal, you are there for four hours."

## Not a typical American player

Mann is the son of parents who both played basketball at Georgia Tech. Their son grew up in Georgia but was not recruited by any Atlantic Coast Conference schools. After one year at Hargrave Military Academy in Virginia, he impressed longtime Belmont coach Rick Byrd, who offered him a roster spot. Mann averaged nearly 18 points per game as senior and was an All-Ohio Valley Conference player.

While hundreds of Division I basketball players head to Europe each year, Mann is not a typical American playing hoops overseas.

For one, he spent considerable time in Europe before he began his pro career. And not only is he married – not all that uncommon – but his wife also has a job for this season at least. Amy Jo is a receptionist at a U.S. military base after volunteering at a coffee shop in Mons that is run by a couple from Texas.

"If I hadn't played soccer or sports at all it would be hard to understand what he is going through, such as a tough loss. We had some tough (soccer) losses at Belmont," said Amy Jo, who also knows there are times to talk about anything but the latest loss.

Mann went to Europe in high school with a low-level USA basketball team and also made a trip to visit his sister in Spain, who was studying abroad. He went to Italy on a mission trip as a freshman at Belmont and then as a sophomore as the Bruins made a basketball trip to Italy. One summer during college he and a friend traveled around Europe.

So when it was clear Mann would not be heading straight from Belmont to the NBA there was no gnashing of teeth.

This season his agent found a job for him in Belgium, a country of about 12 million people that is known for its chocolate, beer and waffles and borders France, Germany, The Netherlands and Luxembourg.

"Someone told me you have not played in Europe until you have been cut," said Mann, 25.

He survived that initial setback, and now he and his wife are provided the free use of a two-bedroom apartment 10 minutes from the basketball arena in Mons.

They have free use of a car, and his monthly salary is deposited into a Belgian bank to do as he wishes, and the club takes care of his Belgian taxes. His American teammates this season have included Justin Cage, who played at Xavier, and Northwestern product Tre Demps.

There are plenty of surprises along the way.

Last season in Germany, he watched as a game ended in tie.

The game between two teams at the bottom of the standings was the first of a home-and-home series that would decide which team would be relegated to a lower division the following season. Since the combined score of both games would decide who would be banished — just like relegation soccer games in Europe — the teams figured the matter would be settled in the second game anyway.

"I went into shock. The last possession the guy (with the ball) really didn't even try to score," Mann said. "It was so un-American."

Another surprise, at least to many Europeans, was the election of Donald Trump.

"They couldn't believe that Trump won. It has definitely been interesting to see the European perspective," Mann said.

These days, as opposed to 15 years ago, American basketball players in Europe can keep in touch with friends and family via Skype. But that still doesn't replace face-to-face contact.

"The biggest challenge is probably missing on family time," Amy Jo said. "I have three older sisters and two of them have kids. You are missing them growing up. My one sister may come and visit in March. My parents have come (to Europe), his parents have come."

Despite the challenges, Mann feels in no hurry to seek a 9-to-5 job or play in a lower-paying minor league in North America.

With two jobs and an English-speaking church to plug into in Mons, the couple has a life not unlike those of friends back home.

"Of course, every player dreams to make it to the highest level and that is the NBA," Mann said. "I was realistic to know it was not going to happen right off the bat. I had my eyes set on Europe, and I have enjoyed it. I will play as long as I can. I would like to ride the basketball wave as long as I can."

### J.J. MANN

**As a pro:** Oberwart (Austria) Gunners (2014-15), Phoenix (Germany) Hagen (2015-16), Belfius (Belgium) Mons-Hainaut (2016-17).

**In college:** Standout at Belmont, where he was named the Ohio Valley Conference Player of the Year, 2013-14.

**Before college:** Played one season at Hargrave Military Academy in Chatham, Va.; played three seasons at Marist (Ga.) High School.

*Update: Mann began this season with a team in Germany.*

# The Fort Wayne Comet

*This story originally ran in the Fort Wayne Sentinel in 2016 and was reprinted with permission.*

Even though he had a standout senior season at Fort Wayne, three-point specialist Max Landis was realistic about his chances for a shot at the National Basketball Association.

"I kind of knew I wasn't going to get drafted," said Landis, 23, who averaged 19.3 points last season with the Mastodons and made 44.7 percent of his three-point attempts.

But the 6-foot-2 guard still secured workouts with four NBA teams: the Chicago

Bulls, Milwaukee Bucks, Indiana Pacers and Utah Jazz after earning the 2015-16 Summit League Player of the Year award.

Following those workouts, his agent told him about a chance to play pro basketball in Belgium, but that meant turning down any opportunity that may have come up in the NBA D-League.

His agent said "it was the best opportunity, so I took it. Right now, I can make more over here than in the D-League," said Landis, standing courtside prior to a recent road game in Antwerp, about a one hour drive northeast of the nation's capital, Brussels.

Landis is a first-year pro with a Belgian team in Aalst, a small city of about 80,000 just northwest of Brussels. Historical records for the city date to the ninth century and the town of Aalst was bombed and occupied by the Germans in both World War I and II, according to published reports.

Landis is provided an apartment and car by the team, as well as a meal allowance, and he lives with his wife, the former Stephanie Mauk, who also played basketball at Fort Wayne.

The couple was married on July 16 and less than a month later they were on their way to Belgium.

"It is completely different than living in the States," said Stephanie, who made the road trip to Antwerp. "Everything is closed down on Sundays. There is always a language barrier since not everyone speaks English."

Recently, she was joined by her parents, Jeff and Amy, who made the trip from the States to watch Landis take on the host Port of Antwerp Giants in a EuroMillions Basketball League game.

The home of the Giants holds about 5,000 fans and was near capacity for a late Sunday afternoon contest.

Landis was in the starting lineup for Aalstar and for much of the first half he had to defend against Giants' point guard Jason Clark, an American, who starred in college at Georgetown and has played overseas for several years.

Landis was one of six Americans on the Aalstar roster, including former Troy player Vernon Taylor, who has playing overseas since 2011.

"He can do the same things he did in college," Taylor said of Landis. "We know (he) is a three-point shooter. "He doesn't have to put so much pressure on himself. Of course, he is young. Everyone hits that rookie wall. He is like a little brother to us; on and off the court he is great guy."

Landis and company came back from a 12-point halftime deficit to win 82-79 and the victory came in front of a small, but loyal and loud, group of fans who made the trek from Aalst, a common occurrence for soccer and basketball supporters for the road team in European leagues.

"In Aalst it is like a family environment," Landis said. "We get a lot of fans on the away games."

Landis is averaging nearly 11 points and two assists per game through his first eight games and he is learning the ways of European basketball away from the gym, as much as in it.

He explained that the use of the provided car, which has the team logo on the side, is decorated so the city residents know he is one of the imports on the team.

So far Landis has been able to make trips to bordering France, Germany, and The Netherlands. Aalstar has also trained in bordering Luxembourg, and Max and Stephanie are planning to spend time in Rome when the team is off for a few days.

So while Landis may not be in the NBA, he is enjoying his first year as a pro athlete overseas and he has no regrets on where his career has taken him so far.

"That was an easy decision," Landis said of bypassing the NBA D-League.

*Update: Landis averaged 17.5 points per game in his first two contests this season for a team in Porto, Portugal.*

# From Georgetown to European Union

*This story originally ran on the athletic website of Georgetown University in 2017 and was reprinted with permission.*

Brussels — Jason Clark dribbled the ball up the court and drove to the basket, connecting on a layup with just less than one minute to play in the fourth quarter as he was fouled.

"Jason Clark!" shouted the public address announcer, sitting in a corner near the baseline of the home team's basket.

Clark, 26, a former Georgetown standout who grew up in northern Virginia, made the free throw and ended the contest with a game-high 36 points.

But the best game of his pro career did not take place in the National Basketball Association or even in the D-League.

While the Hoyas have sent a slew of players to the NBA, Clark is one of several former Georgetown stars who has forged a significant career playing pro hoops in Europe or overseas. He is playing this season in Belgium, where he was leading the league in scoring.

"That was my dream, to play in the NBA," said Clark, who ended his college career in 2012. "It really didn't dawn on me until after my senior year" at Georgetown about playing overseas.

That summer, Clark had a summer workout with the Miami Heat, but it didn't translate into an NBA roster spot. "Calls started coming in from overseas. It was shocking to me. A lot of calls were coming in," he recalls, standing courtside in Antwerp.

Clark began his pro career in Belgium and then played in Germany and Turkey before returning to play for Port of Antwerp in Belgium this season. He was averaging 20 points, four rebounds and four assists per contest through mid-January in a league that requires six Belgians on a 12-man roster.

Belgium is a country of about 12 million people that borders France, Germany,

The Netherlands and Luxembourg. Flemish and French are the main languages in a country that is known for its beer, chocolate and waffles.

Clark is playing in Antwerp, famous for its diamonds and was the final home of famous 17th century painter Peter Paul Rubens. Antwerp is about one-hour north by train from capital Brussels. The home to the European Union, Brussels is a diverse, vibrant city not unlike New York City.

The 6-foot-2 guard wasn't the only Georgetown product playing in Belgium this season. Another one is Brandon Bowman, 32, who ended his Hoyas career in 2006 and has since played from Italy to Serbia to New Zealand. Bowman had 21 points against Clark and Antwerp in November.

"He was one of the players I grew up watching," Clark said of Bowman. "It was nice to catch up with him."

Clark grew up in Woodbridge, Virginia and played in high school at Bishop O'Connell in Arlington in the competitive Washington Catholic Athletic Conference. He went overseas for the first time when the Hoyas visited China during his college days. He gives a lot of credit to Georgetown head coach John Thompson III, who provided direction beyond just hoops, according to Clark.

Clark scored 36 points in this late November game - the most in his overseas career - but Aalstar came back from a 12-point halftime deficit to win 82-79 as Clark missed a 3-pointer in the final seconds after a questionable walk call went against him.

"The ball just happened to be falling for me. I would never say it's the referee's fault that we lost the game," Clark told Belgian reporters who speak English well. "I have to move on to the next game. We can't blame it on the travel call."

Clark was guarded much of the game by American Max Landis, a first-year pro who was the Summit League Player of the Year in 2016 with IPFW. "He is a player. He is very experienced and is very talented," Landis said of Clark. "He picks his spots really well."

Clark graduated from The Hilltop in 2012 with a degree in sociology. He now lives in an apartment in downtown Antwerp a few minutes from Lotto Arena, which seats about 5,000 fans.

"They take care of all of that," said Clark, who is provided a car and apartment. "You don't have to worry about much. They show you around. It is a pretty comfortable life here."

*Upate: Clark averaged 14 points per contest in his first five games for a team in Belarus this season.*

# Mason Grad Played in Belgium

*This story originally ran on the athletic website of George Mason in 2019 and was reprinted by permission.*

Taylor Brown has learned to adjust as a basketball player. After her freshman season at Georgetown, she decided to transfer and she had three standout years at George Mason before graduating in 2016.

But the Bowie, Md., product is now learning to adjust on and off the court in her third season of pro basketball in Europe. After her rookie pro year in Iceland, she has played the past two seasons in Luxembourg.

"I think one of the biggest difference in the rules between NCAA and Europe is when the shot clock goes off here, and say your team does not get their shot off on time before the shot clock goes off, but the ball still touches the rim after the shot clock goes off, the opponent team can just go, take the rebound, and continue playing the game on the offense," according to Brown, 25. "Usually back home in the states, that is considered a turnover, you must stop playing, and the opponent must take the ball out of bounds before resuming the game. The challenge with this was just remembering to keep playing regardless of the shot clock going off."

Brown is a guard who was averaging 23.7 points per game in late February for Residence, her team in Luxembourg. She was playing more than 38 minutes per game in 40-minute contests.

"The town I live in is called Walferdange," she wrote. "It is a nice, small town but I like it a lot because one of my favorite restaurants is right down the street from my apartment which is called the Chocolats du Coeur. A lot of people here in Luxembourg either work at the bank or are teachers. Luxembourg has a lot of nice restaurants such as Chinese, Italian, and Sushi."

"I travel a lot during free time," she added. "I recently just went to Barcelona, Spain. We have two off days during the week which is Monday and Wednesday. I usually travel on Sunday to Monday. Since everything is so close, it is easy to travel to other countries which I love to do. Also, I am a remote video editor for the Prince George's Sentinel (Maryland) newspaper. I edit at least one to two videos per week for the paper, such as high school basketball and football games."

She is also a substitute teacher at the International School of Luxembourg. "So far, I've been a substitute for the Film and Media classes and second grade classes," Brown noted.

Brown was named to the Atlantic 10 All-Conference Third Team in 2016 and ranks second all-time at Mason in scoring, recording 1,693 points in just three years.

So what is a normal day like for Brown in Europe?

"A normal day here in Luxembourg, I wake up around 10 am, I go to Chocolats du Coeur in the morning and eat a crepe and drink a chocolate milkshake, I get shots up at noon with my teammate (the other American), then I go to lunch at the restaurant where we get free lunch, after lunch I usually read or take a nap, then I coach the youth team at 4 pm, after that I have about a hour and thirty minutes to kill before practice at 7 pm. I usually go back to the Chocolats du Coeur before practice and eat a small snack," she noted. "As you can tell, I love chocolate."

She first went overseas in 2016 when she played in Iceland.

"Iceland is a beautiful country and it was really cool I got to see the Northern Lights, a lot from outside my bedroom window and in the city," she wrote.

Along with Brown, Natalie Butler, the A-10 Player of the Year in 2018 for the Patriots, played a few games in Belgium last fall before returning to the states. The Lake Braddock High standout was a third-round pick of Atlanta in the WNBA draft last year. Forward Kristi Mokube, who played alongside Brown at Mason from 2014-16, also played three years overseas in Germany, Greece and Australia.

Among the former Mason men who have been at the pro level overseas this season include Will Thomas (Spain), Darryl Monroe (South Korea), Cameron Long (Israel), Isaiah Tate (Canada), Mike Morrison (Germany), Ryan Pearson (France), Bryon Allen (Italy), Jonathan Arledge (Latvia), Jalen Jenkins (Bulgaria) and Daniel Baptista (Portugal), according to eurobasket.com.

Monroe was averaging nearly 20 points per game in South Korea while Pearson and Allen were playing in two of the top leagues in western Europe. A Baltimore native, Thomas, who was a member of the Final Four team in 2006, has also played in Belgium, Georgia, Turkey and Italy in a pro career that began in 2008.

*Update: Brown averaged 14 points per game in her first 12 contests this season for a team in Sweden. Butler began the 2021-22 season with a team in Greece.*

# Brother of NBA Star Forges Own Path

*This story originally ran in the Goshen alumni magazine in 2019 and was reprinted by permission.*

Kazan, Russia — Errick McCollum '10 had the basketball at the top of the key and sank a 3-pointer, giving his team a seven-point lead they would not relinquish. That long-distance bomb ignited a large puff of smoke above his team's basket, and fans of the green-clad Unics of Kazan — a professional basketball team in Kazan, Russia, that plays in the VTB United League and EuroCup — roared their approval. A banner in Russian a few feet behind the basket said "We are Together" in both English and Russian. Another sign in English said "While I breathe, I hope and believe in my team."

That devotion to the local club — be it soccer or basketball — is not uncommon in Europe and other parts of the world. There is also some quirkiness to basketball overseas, as McCollum has discovered in nine years of a vagabond existence that has taken him from Turkey to China and this season to Russia for play in the top league in that country.

"Basketball is such a global sport," he said, standing on the court in Kazan after a game this season.

Over the years, several other Goshen College men's basketball players have also gone on to play the sport professionally overseas after graduation as well, though McCollum has seen the most success. He has helped lead his team Overseas Elite to four consecutive championship wins in the annual The Basketball Tournament and he set a record in the Chinese professional league in 2015 for the most points in a game with 82 when he played for the Zhejiang Golden Bulls.

## Coming to Goshen

McCollum, 31, grew up in Canton, Ohio and dealt mostly with two cultures — African-American and Caucasian. That changed when he got to Goshen. "It allowed me to see different cultures," he said. "Goshen introduced me to different cultures and people. I was a bit close-minded back then, but [at GC] I met students from different countries who changed my perspective. I began to immerse myself in other cultures beside my own. Those friends I met taught me about their traditions."

"What I appreciated about Errick was his loyalty to Goshen College and his teammates. He could have transferred to a higher level after his [first] year when there was a coaching change, but instead he decided to stay and finish out his career at Goshen," said Gary Chupp, former men's basketball head coach.

## A Global Career

After a standout college performance — he holds the single season and career scoring records in men's basketball, and in his senior year one of his dunks made it on to ESPN SportsCenter's Top 10 plays — he graduated in 2010 with a degree in business. Since then, he has seen the world through basketball, also playing for teams in Greece and Israel.

"I enjoy seeing different places/ cultures, going somewhere new and just adapting," he said. "Each country is a new adventure and every place has something historic or a sight to behold. I've been blessed to see many places. I've visited 20 different countries so far through basketball."

"God blessed me with the ability and talent to play basketball," he added. "I took that gift, worked extremely hard and maximized it. Yes, it's true not many guys coming from smaller colleges play at the professional level, but when God has something for you, nothing can get in the way of that. Here I am nine years into my career, just blessed. I just try and glorify God's name and represent my family and everything associated with me in a positive manner."

The 6-foot, 1-inch McCollum had several teammates this season in Russia who had impressive Division I pedigrees and even some NBA experience, but it was McCollum who played point guard in key stretches for the team in Kazan.

"He is an amazing player," said his teammate, Jordan Carmichael. "He brings all the things you would want in a teammate in Europe. He's selfless, very skilled and can play the one and two guard spots and is the best shooter I have ever been around. He is very talented and such a veteran leader, which helps me so much on and off the court."

McCollum has gotten used to adapting to new countries and cultures. That was also true in Kazan, which is about 500 miles east of Moscow and has about 1.2 million people.

## Leaving a Legacy Off the Court

"Life in Kazan is a little like the Midwest," he said. "Except it's colder and more snow."

McCollum's brother, C.J., was a star at Division I Lehigh University and is now a standout in the NBA with the Portland Trailblazers. They have remained close and both try to be role models off the court.

Last fall the brothers teamed up with an Akron, Ohio food bank for their first annual turkey giveaway to provide Thanksgiving meals for 200 families. They also host a summer youth basketball camp in Akron, mentoring more than 100 kids in their hometown.

"My brother and I talk almost every day," the Goshen grad said. "We watch and keep up with each other's games, and push each other on and off the court. He's my little brother, my workout buddy, business partner all in one. We have a very unique relationship that has pushed us to excel at an extremely high level on the court, but what I'm most proud of is the difference that we have been able to make off the court."

*Update: McCollum was still in Russia playing pro hoops to begin the 2021-22 season.*

# Career Abroad for Xavier Standouts

*This story originally ran in the alumni magazine of Xavier 15 years ago and is reprinted by permission.*

Torraye Braggs is becoming an expert in world geography. The 1998 graduate and former standout with the men's basketball team was selected in the second round of the National Basketball League draft by the Utah Jazz, but he has spent most of his career making a scenic tour of Europe, South America and Asia.

His goal: to find a place to keep showcasing his on-court talents. Although he returned to the States in December to play in the NBA's Development League, he spent the beginning of the season in South Korea, while previous ventures led him to teams in Russia, Spain, Greece, Israel, Puerto Rico and Venezuela.

Braggs, however, isn't alone in his world travels. While the list of former Musketeers playing in the NBA is growing, the list of those making a living playing basketball in professional leagues overseas is just as long. Anthony Myles, for instance, began this season playing in China, as did Reggie Butler. Romain Sato now plays in Italy and Pete Sears in Finland. Kevin Frey played in Germany last year before returning to the States to play for a Development League team in New Mexico. Michael Hawkins played in Spain last year before moving to a team in Syria in the fall. Lionel Chalmers, a second-round draft pick of the Los Angeles Clippers, now plays for a team in Greece.

When the limitations of NBA rosters prove too much but the desire to play the game—and get paid to do it—hasn't diminished, heading overseas is a common destination for many former college standouts. It's a great opportunity to see the world while at the same time further developing the skills that might land them in the NBA.

Most Americans who play in Europe are provided the free use of an apartment and car, and some get meal allowances. Most of them have very little expenses, and the host club normally pays the players' taxes in that country. Top stars can make more than $500,000 in countries such as Spain and Italy. Top Americans in Hungary can make nearly $100,000, while first-year Americans in countries such as Germany and Austria may have a salary around $40,000 a season.

But, it certainly has its challenges.

"The biggest adjustment to playing overseas is the culture and the way of life—the languages, food, rules, how they do things, how they live, their thoughts of Americans," says Myles, who has also played in Spain and Turkey. "As far as on the court, their rules of the game and their style of play are different. For example, in Spain it's about the team—who is in the best shape and has the better players. Here in China, the top teams run the fastest because they are not strong enough to play one-on-one."

Myles began this season with the Guangdong Southern Tigers, a team in the Canton province near Hong Kong and the south China Sea. He's one of about 56.5 million people in the province, although the 6-foot-9 African American is certainly one of the most noticeable. "Well, being black here, a lot of the Chinese people are scared of us," he says. "I don't know why. They are always watching us no matter where we are and what we are doing. They follow us around, but they are scared to talk to us if we say something to them."

Still, he hasn't allowed that to affect his play. In his first game, he had 31 points and 15 rebounds. In his second game, he had 48 points and 16 rebounds, the most points he ever scored in a game at any level. He joined the team after playing in the first division in Spain, which many American players say is the best league outside of the NBA.

Sato, a second-round draft pick of the San Antonio Spurs in 2004, is also making an impact, leading his team in scoring in the B league in Italy, which is considered one of the best in Europe. Sears, too, is doing well, averaging 13 points per game in his first five contests in Finland.

Being overseas does not mean that the NBA dream is over. James Singleton from Murray State University, who played the past two seasons in Italy, is a rookie this year with the NBA's L.A. Clippers.

Myles and others are well aware of that. In addition to spending his free time playing video games and watching movies, he likes "keeping tabs on the NBA games and season, because it is my dream to some day be playing in the league."

*Update: Former Xavier standout Malcolm Bernard averaged more than 17 points per game for a team in Russia in his first 11 games this season. At least two former Explorers were with teams in Germany earlier this season: Semaj Christon, drafted by Miami in 2014, and Quentin Goodwin, who was with the Bayer Giants.*

# Rookie From Davidson Finds a Home

*This story originally appeared in the alumni magazine of Davidson College in 2019 and was reprinted with permission.*

Lisbon — Mackenzie Latt was still feeling the effects of a transatlantic flight, arriving in Europe for the first time just a few hours earlier. Now the former Davidson basketball star was scrimmaging with her new team in Portugal, which like most European leagues expects big-time performances from its American imports.

"I was feeling a little bit out of whack. I was like a fish out of water," Latt says, sitting in a pastry shop in downtown Lisbon a few months later. "I was completely lost. You feel like you are in a little bubble [without knowing the language]."

Latt had to adapt to new rules and was surrounded by a language and culture that was totally foreign to her. But that was part of her personal challenge, as she vowed to continue her basketball career after the Wildcats were eliminated from the Atlantic 10 Conference tournament in her final college game last March.

"At the end of the day I wanted an adventure," said Latt, who graduated with a degree in communications in 2018.

She certainly got one, arriving in a country she knew little about.

Her agent, who had seen her play at a tournament in Ohio, laid out possible first-year pro stops in Luxembourg, England and Czech Republic. She decided on Portugal, partially due to the veteran coach she had heard good things about, the warm weather and the relatively small size of the country.

Latt has taken advantage of budget airlines in Europe to explore other countries.

"So far I have gone to Madrid and London," she said, sitting in the Lisbon café in mid-January. "Sometimes we have weekends off and I have really tried to take advantage of those when I can. It has been empowering to go on a day trip on your own, as silly as that sounds."

The 6-foot-1 Latt survived those rough first few days, scoring a season-high 26 points in her second pro game in Portugal.

"To have a little bit of a breakthrough game so early, I was so thankful," she said. "It was a reassuring moment and it was like 'you are where you are supposed to be.' I think we ended up winning in overtime. To be able to contribute to a very good team win was reassuring and a little bit calming."

Latt's experienced several "ah-ha" moments off the court as well, living far from her family. She was able to share her new life with her parents, who visited Portugal last year. Her mother played basketball at the University of Toledo, in Ohio.

## New Experiences

Latt averaged at least 10 points per game in all four seasons with the Wildcats, and scored 14.9 points and grabbed 8.2 rebounds per game as a senior in 2017-18 when she was named third-team all-Atlantic 10 Conference while playing for head coach Gayle Coats Fulks.

In her first 14 games at the pro level with Lombos Quinta in Portugal she averaged 10.7 points and 5.4 boards per contest.

Latt is one three Davidson women who are playing pro hoops overseas this winter. The others are Katrin Chiemeka and Sofija Aleksandravicius, who both ended their Davidson careers during the 2012-13 season. Chiemeka is playing in her native France, while Aleksandravicius, who went to high school in New York, is playing in Krakow, Poland. She was the Southern Conference defensive player of the year in 2012 and 2013.

A high school standout in Michigan, Latt said Davidson prepared her for life overseas on and off the court.

"Davidson is all about new experiences, being put out of your comfort zone in order to grow," she said. "I have been told I am one of the more adaptable players they have seen, which I take as high praise."

It is not unusual for Americans, both men and women, to have careers of at least 10 years overseas with pro basketball. Latt said she sees herself perhaps playing a few years as a pro.

So what would Latt be doing if she was not playing overseas?

"That is a good question," she said. "I am definitely considering the grad assistant route. I would like to go back to school; the question is what would I study. I think I could do well in public relations. I could see myself as a coach. I love sports, it would be fun to stay around it."

For now she is playing a few miles from Lisbon and enjoying a country of about 11 million people, where many speak some English. She was the only American on her team for part of the season before Kansas native Merissa Quick joined the team in October. Latt has her own apartment and relies on public transportation.

"I am here to play basketball but I am also here for the experience and to explore and to be on my own and try new things," she said. "I could see myself doing this one or two more years maybe. But I am close to my family and close to my friends. I would hate to miss out on things by being here, which sometimes seems a world away."

*Update: Latt played just one season in Portugal. Davidson's Chloe Johnson, who is from Arizona, played in England during the 2019-20 season.*

# Seeing the World After William & Mary

*This story was originally used for the athletic website at William & Mary in 2019 and was reprinted with permission.*

Warsaw — Omar Prewitt had only been in basketball-crazy Lithuania for a few days, and his first time in Europe was wearing on his psyche.

"It's cold, it's snowy. I had to wake up 20 minutes early for practice just to scrape the snow off my car every day. I didn't know if I was going to make it. But then I settled in," he said of his first experience with pro basketball overseas. "I am from Kentucky so I am used to basketball culture; they are crazy about it."

But the former Tribe basketball standout did survive that first pro season, playing in 14 games in Lithuania during the 2017-18 campaign before moving to Greece, where he averaged 5.5 points per contest in 15 A1 league contests there.

Prewitt has built on that challenging first pro season.

He began this season with a team in Warsaw, the capital of Poland that was heavily bombed during World War II. Picking up a few words of Polish and learning about its checkered history is part of the territory for Prewitt, who has excelled on the court with a season-high 36 points on January 12.

Prewitt, who graduated in 2017 with a degree in kinesiology, was averaging 17.5 points per contest though the opening 20 games for Legia and was named the player of the month for Poland's top league in November. For most of the season, he has been the only American on his team in a competitive world of pro hoops in Europe.

"The craziest thing about pro basketball here is no one is safe," said the 6-foot-7 Prewitt, 24, sitting in the lobby of a hotel in downtown Warsaw. "I have seen coaches moved like that. I have seen players moved just like that. If they are going to bring you all the way from America, you are going to be one of the highest paid players on the court and you are expected to score. That is the perception of us."

David Cohn is in his first season with a pro league in Israel with a team in Eilat, home to about 50,000 people.

"I am in the southern part of the country on the Red Sea," he said in a telephone interview in late January.

"I'm five minutes from Jordan and 10 minutes from Egypt. It's amazing."

Terry Tarpey, who was born in France, is in his third season in the country. He led Le Mans to its fifth French National Basketball League Championship. Primarily a starter, he averaged nearly seven points and five rebounds in 2018.

"The town where I play, Le Mans, would compare well with a small city in the states," according to Tarpey. "There's 250,000 people in the area, with probably about 150,000 downtown and the other 100,000 in the suburbs. There is a famous cathedral in my town and I often walk by it on my way to my favorite crepery for lunch. It's called Saint Julien's Cathedral and is massive, beautiful, and still a functioning church."

## Hoops Beyond the CAA Tournament

With the CAA tournament drawing near in South Carolina, the achievements of Prewitt, Cohn and others show that a basketball career doesn't have to end once their last game with the Tribe is in the record books.

Prewitt is one of several former Tribe hoopsters who has played basketball overseas this winter.

Former William & Mary women's standout and Virginia Beach native Jazmen Boone, who ended her college career in 2015, played in Australia last year after two seasons in Ireland. Emily Correal, after stops in Italy, Switzerland and Sweden, was signed by a team in January in Belgium. Kaitlyn Mathieu played in a few games in Bulgaria last fall after earlier gigs in Germany, Denmark, Macedonia and Luxembourg. After graduating last year, Abby Rendle played in Belgium this year.

Other products of coach Tony Shaver's program overseas this season include former CAA Player of the Year Marcus Thornton, who was in Turkey before suffering an injury; Oliver Tot (Slovakia), Laimis Kisielius in his native Lithuania; Thomas Papas (Greece), Cohn (Israel), Tarpey (France), Daniel Dixon, who played in France before joining the Northern Arizona Suns of the G-League, and Connor Burchfield, who is also in the G-League with the Greensboro Swarm

Dixon played in the summer league with the Boston Celtics in 2018 before heading to Europe. Burchfield was a first-round pick in the G-League Draft in 2018 by the Austin Spurs before spending time with the Sioux Falls SkyForce and the Swarm.

Thornton was drafted in the second round by the Boston Celtics in 2015 out of college and previously played in Australia, Italy and China. Tot was born in Hungary and grew up in Slovakia and averaged nearly nine points per contest in his first 22 games this season. In total, Kisielius has played 11 seasons in Europe with stops in Ukraine, Latvia, Germany and Belarus along with playing in Lithuania.

Tarpey was the two-time CAA Defensive Player of the Year during his W&M career and recorded the first triple-double in program history. He now has the opportunity to play professionally for the same organization his farther did after a standout career at NYU.

"Before starting my journey to play professional basketball I lived overseas for 3 years, the first 3 years of my life, in the very town that I'm in now. My father played professional basketball in France for 10 years, and I was born the year before he changed teams to Le Mans, where he finished his career. I don't remember much, and the language certainly didn't stick around after we moved back to New York in 1997," Tarpey noted.

Cohn's father has Jewish heritage and that aided his decision to play pro ball in Israel. He does not count against the limit of North Americans on the team.

"I have always wanted to play professional basketball, it had been a dream of mine," according to Cohn. "Most decisions I made growing up revolved around the idea of which would set me up to achieve that dream the best. From last March 'til now, I signed with my agents at Beyond Athlete Management, worked tirelessly all summer in the gym and signed my deal for Israel while I was with the Philadelphia 76ers summer league training camp. I had been outside of the U.S. a few times, but never to Israel. At first it was different than any place I had been but it's grown on me tremendously."

Cohn graduated from W&M as the program's all-time leader in assists, playing just three seasons in Williamsburg. He capped his career earning All-CAA honors as a senior, before starting his professional career with the NBA's Philadelphia 76ers over the summer.

"As a rookie the biggest adjustments for me on the court has to be the physicality of the league," Cohn added. "First off you're playing 30-year-old and plus men and 17 different guys who have NBA experience in the league. The way the game is refereed is also completely different. As a point guard also the way you operate in pick and roll situations is also different. But with every week that goes by I feel like it's becoming easier to understand how to play here. Off the court, I spend a lot of time alone which gets lonely. Thank God for Apple and their FaceTime so I can 'see' family and friends regularly. I have a lot of free time as well, so learning how to adequately spend that time has taken some time."

### Tribe Program Helped Pave the Way

Prewitt was part of a Tribe program that advanced to the CAA title game twice in his career. He averaged 15.6 points and 6.2 rebounds per game as a senior for William & Mary during the 2016-17 season and was a second-team All-CAA player.

The top Polish league requires six Polish players on each team and two have to be on the court at all times. Like most Americans playing in Europe he is provided the free use of a car and apartment and has very few expenses.

"Our Polish guys are very good. They contribute to our team very well," Prewitt said. "Our coaches are from Macedonia and one of them is Polish. All of them speak very good English. All of the players speak English; you almost have to if you want to play since Americans are going to be the focal point of most teams. The language barrier is very easy within the team."

Cohn was teammates with Prewitt and graduated last year with degrees in history and kinesiology.

"I owe so much to William and Mary and all the people that make it such a special place," wrote Cohn. "The rigorous class work taught me many lessons especially time management. More importantly, it taught me you get out what you put in. The faculty at WM is second to none in my opinion. The basketball program helped me demonstrate my abilities to the highest level, and helped me prepare mentally for the grind of being a professional basketball player. I truly cannot say enough positive things about both academics and athletics at W&M and how much it already has and will continue to help me excel moving forward in my professional career."

Prewitt has been around basketball since he was a young boy. His mother, Lea, played at the University of Kentucky and coached both of his sisters at Centre College in Kentucky.

So how long would Prewitt like to play overseas? "I told myself coming out of college I would have a three-year plan," he said. "If I am making a certain amount after my third year I would like to keep playing. I want to have a family when I am grown up, too. I know I have opportunities back home. This summer I will get my real estate license; that is what my dad does. It is a great backup."

For now he is enjoying his second season overseas.

Prewitt was the only American on his team in late January, and he had teammates from London, Russia, Belarus as well as Poland. "It is cool to get to know those guys and their experiences growing up and how they were different from mine," he said.

*Update: Prewitt began this season with a team in Bamberg, Germany.*

# DePaul Product Has Been All Over

*This story originally ran in The Washington Times in 2019 and is reprinted by permission.*

Starograd Gdanski — With the clock winding down, Baltimore native Cleveland Melvin connected on a shot from the top of the key, pumping his fist as his late heroics helped MKS Dabrowa Gornicza to a road win in the top Polish pro basketball league.

The former DePaul player has scored more than 1,500 points in a globe-trotting pro career that began in 2014 and has included, in addition to Poland, stints in Hungary, Israel, Mexico, Thailand, Croatia and even Lebanon.

"I didn't feel in danger," the 6-foot-8 Melvin said of his time in the Middle East. "I stayed in my apartment and with my team. I was not in bad areas. I was more in the gym and staying in my space."

Melvin, who averaged double-digit scoring in four seasons at DePaul, is one of dozens of basketball players from the Baltimore-Washington region now playing overseas.

Managing an international basketball career isn't easy for the American players who choose that path, but it can be even tougher on loved ones back home.

It's true, says Carla Arrington, whose son, Rodney Glasgow Jr., played at Good Counsel High in Montgomery County and Virginia Military Institute. Since 2014, Glasgow has played in Switzerland and Belgium, and he's now in his second season with a team in Slovakia.

"I worry about his safety because of everything happening in the world right now," said Arrington, who lives in Waldorf, Maryland.

It's worth noting there were more than 150 homicides in the District in 2018 — and 57 murders in all of Slovakia.

"I can't help it. He will always be my baby," Arrington texted.

Glasgow, 26, and his mother are close and communicate at least once a week, using the messaging app WhatsApp. The 5-foot-11 guard averaged 9.0 points per game in his first 21 games this season for Prievidza in the top Slovakian league.

"Honestly, I've been fortunate to play in countries where I don't have to worry about (my safety)," Glasgow said in an email. "The only concern is getting through customs. But I'd rather be in Europe than in my own country with all our problems being a black man and seeing what it's done to people who look like me, or minorities for that matter."

Omar Prewitt, once a standout at William & Mary, played in hoop-crazy Lithuania and Greece last season in his first year overseas. His parents were visiting him in Greece last season when a riot and protest took place on the street near where his parents were staying. But his parents were safe, as they watched the action up high from their apartment balcony after being tipped by a local to stay inside for a few hours.

This year, Prewitt is with a team in the Polish capital of Warsaw.

"I personally don't (fear) for my safety," said Prewitt, sitting in a hotel lobby in downtown Warsaw.

Ben Richardson, who helped Loyola of Chicago to its magical Final Four run last spring, is also a first-year pro in Poland on the same team as Melvin.

"The biggest thing is you to come in with an open mind," he said. "I didn't know anything about Poland."

Glasgow said adapting is key.

"The biggest challenge I had playing on the court overseas, would be adjusting to the European game," he noted. "The language barrier can also be something if you have a coach who can't speak English really well. The same goes for teammates, he said, because every country's teams will have their own local players on the squad.

"So, respecting everyone's culture is a key," Glasgow said.

Many American players have to decide whether to play minor league ball at home or go overseas. The advantage to staying in the U.S. is being closer to family and friends and, if playing for a G League team, being readily available for an NBA call-up.

But playing overseas, especially in western European leagues, China or Russia, can mean a much better salary.

"The minuses are you might not be used to being overseas. You have to adjust to everything," Melvin said, acknowledging the lifestyle isn't for everyone. "You have to make that important decision in your career."

*Update: Melvin was back in Hungary for the 2021-22 season before he was released in November.*

# From Buffalo to the Balkans

*This story originally ran in the Laurel Leader of Maryland in 2019 and was reprinted by permission.*

Belgrade — Each spring the National Basketball Association holds its annual player draft, and for the past few years that has consisted of just 60 selections. And not every player drafted makes the roster of his NBA team that season.

Throw in non-drafted free agents, who sign with a team, and there are perhaps one or two spots that open each season with an NBA team.

With few opportunities in the NBA, many American players, with a Division I history, head overseas each year to begin a pro career.

Two players with ties to Laurel have played in Europe this season: Rodney Glasgow, Jr. has been in Slovakia while David Kadiri has been in Serbia.

Kadiri lived in Laurel as a teenager and played at Coolidge High in Washington, D.C. for head coach Vaughn Jones, a former standout at DeMatha Catholic High in Hyattsville and at George Washington University.

As a freshman, Kadiri played at the University of Maryland, Baltimore County and saw action in 27 games, with 10 starts.

Kadiri went on to play at South Plains Junior College before committing to the University of Buffalo. He finished his college career in 2017 at Buffalo and was part of a team that won the Mid-American Conference title in 2016.

Last season, he played in England for the Manchester Giants in his first season overseas.

The Germantown native has played this winter in Uzice, Serbia.

The town of about 60,000 people in western Serbia is the home of several notable soccer and basketball players and was heavily bombed by NATO forces in 1999.

"I am playing in Uzicé which is a pretty small town in Serbia surrounded by mountains," he wrote from Serbia. "It's pretty nice, tranquil, and the people here love basketball. In my free time I love going to to the coffee shops. I go sightseeing in the mountains, and I also have my 4-month old pitbull terrior with me so he keeps me company as well."

Kadiri, a 6-foot-7 forward, averaged nearly 10 points and 4.5 rebounds in his first 19 games this season in Serbia. He had a season-high 27 points on Feb. 2 in a win over Beovuk 72.

"Playing basketball after college was something I was always interested in," according to Kadiri. "I had an interesting two years at Buffalo and just kind of battling partial tear in my quadriceps tendon and playing through that. A lot of rehab and perseverance I was still able to overcome that, enjoy my time there, win a MAC championship with them, and still pursue professional basketball."

There are more than 100 Serbian men playing basketball at colleges and at the pro level this winter in the United States, according to EuroBasket.com.

One of the Serbian players in the NBA is Nikola Jokic, who is averaging 20.4 points, 10.5 rebounds and 7.7 assists for the NBA's Denver Nuggets.

"The biggest difference I notice from NCAA and Europe ball would be the different pace and just the style of play," noted Kadiri, one of just 10 or so Americans to play in the pro league in Serbia this season.

Rodney Glasgow Jr., who spent part of his youth growing up in Laurel, is playing professionally in Slovakia after playing collegiately at Virginia Military Institute.

Glasgow spent part of his youth in Laurel and Odenton and attended The Bullis School in Potomac before transferring to Good Counsel in Olney so he could play in the Washington Catholic Athletic Association.

Point guard Glasgow, 26, headed overseas after playing in the fast-paced offense for head coach Duggar Baucom at Virginia Military Institute in Lexington, Virginia through 2014.

He played in Switzerland and Belgium and has spent the past two seasons in Slovakia.

"I always knew I wanted to play basketball professionally, but my senior year was when I really decided to accept going overseas. My college coach told me he would help me get there if I committed and he kept his word all the way," Glasgow wrote from Slovakia. "Love coach Baucom (now at The Citadel). And it was just my family getting ready for it. I think they were worried and nervous the first time but they are fine now and always supported me."

What are the biggest challenges of playing in Europe?

"The biggest challenge I had playing on the court overseas, would be adjusting to the European game," according to Glasgow. "You have to be efficient at your position, and have IQ offensively and defensively at a quicker speed especially as a guard. The language barrier can also be something if you have a coach who can't speak English really well when they break down plays or a game plan."

"And teammates, because every country will have their local players and imports can be from anywhere. So, respecting everyone's culture is a key. Off the court I would say just being in a different country alone. It makes you mature faster and you have to adjust to the time, food, language, and how the life is. That's why some guys can't do it."

Mikal Cekovsky, who is from Slovakia, played for the Terps of Maryland from 2014 to 2018.

He is now playing as a pro in his native Slovakia but is not on the same team as Glasgow, one of about 25 American men to play in a pro league in Slovakia in the last two seasons, according to EuroBasket.com.

Glasgow is playing in Prievidza, a town of about 50,000 in central-western Slovakia. He was averaging 9.0 points and 2.6 assists in early February.

*Update: Glasgow was averaging about 12 points per game earlier this season for his team in Sheffield, England.*

# Saint Joseph's Alum Persevered

*This story originally ran on the athletic website of Saint Joseph's of Philadelphia in 2013 and was reprinted by permission.*

Frankfurt — After ending his basketball career at Saint Joseph's in 2008, Rob Ferguson had a tryout with the Philadelphia 76ers. "The workout went good and they called me back again," reflect Ferguson, a 6-foot-8 inside presence. Ferguson was optimistic about a second tryout with the NBA team. "I spoke to the GM and the coach and they liked my shooting ability but suggested I go overseas," recalls Ferguson, who had averaged 11.9 points and 4.8 rebounds to help the Hawks earn a bid to the NCAA Tournament his senior year.

While disappointed that his NBA dream did not come true, Ferguson took the advice of the 76ers even though he had never been to Europe.

Personal reasons meant he had to sit out the 2008-09 pro season, so the Florida product began his overseas sojourn the following year as he played for the Giants of Noerdlingen in Germany.

Now, some five years after his college career ended, Ferguson has played for pay in Uruguay and Iceland and last year helped another German team, Vechta, win the Pro A league title as he tallied nearly six points and five boards per outing.

Prior to this season Ferguson signed a two-year contract with Karlsruhe, his third German team, and he began the season in late September. "The game is a lot slower" in Europe, he notes. "They are more plays called than on-on-one (offense). It is more technical."

Located in southwest Germany, Karlsruhe is a city of about 300,000 people that was founded in 1715 and is the birthplace of several top soccer (football) stars.

"Karlsruhe is a bike city. Everyone rides a bike here," says Ferguson, speaking from Germany following a practice session. "It is the biggest city I have played in."

Ferguson is one of several former Hawks who have kept their hoop dreams alive in foreign lands. That includes Pat Calathes, who averaged 17.5 points per game as a senior for the Hawks in 2007-08; Darrin Govens, who averaged 13.9 points as a senior 2010; and Ahmad Nivins, who was the Atlantic 10 Player of the Year in 2009.

Calathes, who is of Greek descent, has played several years in Greece and spent the 2012-13 season in Israel. He has signed to play this season in Kazakhstan, according to eurobasket.com.

A 6-foot-1 guard, Govens has also played pro ball in Iceland and Israel and is lacing up his sneakers this season for a team in Greece.

Nivins, who was drafted by the Dallas Mavericks in 2009, went to Spain and suffered a knee injury. Since recovering, he has played in Belgium and in France, where he was an All-Star last season. This year he will be playing for another team in France, Pau-Lacq-Orthez, after he averaged around 15 points and six boards per contest last season.

Ferguson's German team played in a pre-season tournament in Switzerland in September and basketball has also taken the native of Casselberry, Fla. to France and the Czech Republic. His teammates, in addition to Germans, have included those from Lithuania, Russia, Poland and the Czech Republic.

Other former American NCAA players on the roster of his German team in early October included Jeremy Black (University of Tampa), Andre Calvin (Drake) and Jaivon Harris (Ohio).

Basketball overseas can be a vagabond existence for many Americans, moving from one country to another in search of better competition and, perhaps, a bigger paycheck. But Ferguson appears to be putting down roots: he was married on July 20, 2013 to the former Verena Nickel, who has played women's basketball at a high level in her native country, most recently for DJK Brose Bamberg.

Ferguson, who graduated in 2008 with a degree in fine arts, tells his friends in Florida they should play overseas if they have a chance. Like most Americans with a Division I pedigree, Ferguson is provided the free use of an apartment and transportation by his club in Germany, along with his salary.

Many American males in Germany can make between $1300 to $3200 per month though there is room for flexibility, according to a source. "We (a Pro-A second division team) have some Americans making $1500 a month and others making $3200 a month," according to the source.

Some of the adjustments Ferguson has to make on the court is that FIBA, the governing board of European hoops, will call walking on a player if he does not clearly put the ball on the floor before picking up his pivot foot.

Another transition is that many teams in Europe practice twice a day and sometimes play only once a week. While in Uruguay his team would sometimes practice three times a day – but making the switch is worth it for Ferguson.

"You are living out your dreams if you have a chance to play. It is not like the NBA but you are still playing ball. You are paid to do something you love. If you love what you are doing you never have to work," he says.

*Update: Govens played for Szeged, Hungary in 2020-21 and began the current season with Cholet, in France.*

# Santa Clara and Olympic Ties

*This story originally ran in the alumni magazine of Santa Clara in California in 2005 and was reprinted with permission.*

Uwe Sauer played for the German men's basketball team in the 1984 Summer Olympics in Los Angeles. He then stayed in California and entered Santa Clara that fall as a freshman, and was a member of the men's basketball team.

The next season his teammate was Jens-Uwe Gordon, and now some two decades later Sauer is Gordon's coach for Karlsruhe in the top professional league in Germany. Sauer said that Gordon gets kidded about that relationship sometimes when he is back home in California.

"I have known him for 20 seasons now," Sauer says of Gordon, 37, during a pre-season tournament in Hungary. "Most likely he will finish up (his career) with us. In his head, he is still young. He is still on fire the way he approaches the game. He is a veteran and knows the game. He is a fighter. He keeps the guys together."

How intense is Gordon? While sitting on the bench during a pre-season game this past October, he shouted "Baseline! Baseline!" to his teammates who were on defense midway through the fourth quarter. A few minutes later, he hollered "rebound!" with his team clinging to a two-point lead with 4:31 left in the game.

The 6-foot-9 Gordon, whose mother is from Germany, was born in Salinas. He played four years for the Broncos, and averaged 16.8 points and 8.3 rebounds per game as a senior in 1988-89. He has played professionally in Europe for more than 10 years, and this is his third straight season in Germany.

Gordon and Sauer are just two of SCU's overseas basketball connection. Other former Santa Clara players who began this season outside North America include Brian Jones (Tubingen, Germany), Marlon Garnett (Treviso, Italy) and Jason Sedlock (Mt. Gambier in Australia). Also, SC products who played last season overseas were Brendan Graves (Austria), Jamie Holmes (Netherlands), Harold Keeling (Venezuela) and Steve Ross (France).

Garnett scored 12 points for his Italian team Benetton Treviso, one of the best clubs in Europe, in an 86-83 exhibition game loss against the Toronto Raptors on Oct. 20 in Canada before more than 10,000 fans. But the NBA is a long way off for many former NCAA standouts that head to Europe.

Sedlock, from Oregon, just finished his fifth season in the Australian Basketball League. The season in Australia runs from February to August, and Sedlock considers the caliber of play to similar to that of the West Coast Conference. He majored in political science and received a bachelor of science degree, with a minor in general business, in 1997.

"Santa Clara has helped me tremendously (for) living in another culture," Sedlock wrote in late October, before heading back to Australia for his sixth season. "Many times, the sport is the easy part. It's adjusting to everything else that take patience and the right attitude. Santa Clara opened up my mind to see other cultures from their point of view and not judge them regarding to the American lifestyle."

"On the court Santa Clara taught me to never become complacent," Sedlock added. "Coach (Dick) Davey always preached to us, 'You are getting better or getting worse. You are never staying the same.' "

What is the biggest overseas challenge for Jones, who finished his career at SC in 2001?

"The first thing I have to mention is the language. That was the first adjustment I had to deal with," Jones says from his apartment in southern Germany. "I can now understand a lot of what they are saying, but I can't say what I want to say to them."

Jones, one of two Americans on his team, said another challenge has been the lifestyle. He lives in a town of about 90,000 people about two hours from Munich.

"In America we are used to having everything convenient for us. The 7-11 is open 24 hours a day. In Germany, it is not like that," he says. "In Germany, on Sunday the market is closed. You can't go out to eat at 2 a.m. if you are hungry. The banks are closed from 12 to 2 p.m. (weekdays). You have to plan stuff out a little more."

Sedlock said some of the biggest challenges overseas is dealing with broken promises, monetary issues, or when team management is trying to take advantage of him. And what about being so far from home?

"I don't feel like I get too homesick while I'm playing overseas," he says. "I find it creeps in when I have too (much) downtime on my hands. I've learned to try to keep myself busy learning new things that the opportunity presents," such as learning to play the guitar.

Jones is provided a two-bedroom apartment and a car by his team, which is standard for Americans who play in Europe. His team won the B league title last season and moved up to the A league this season, and that meant that Jones' tax-free salary also rose: he said he receives about the league average for Americans in Germany's top league, around $50,000 to $60,000 American money.

Jones, meanwhile, and other former NCAA players have to adjust their games overseas.

"The game is different in that they don't let you play as aggressive on defense. That was one thing I had to adjust to in my game," he says. "In America, we play with our feet but we also use our hands (on defense). Here, you can't use your hands" unless you want to be called for a foul.

It was Sauer who played a key role in Jones' arrival to Germany as a rookie pro three seasons ago. Jones, who graduated in 2001 with a degree in sociology, played for Sauer his first year in Europe. Sauer then switched German teams after that season.

Jones, unlike German-born Sauer, is a long way from home. But he says there are some things that seem familiar.

"My town (in Germany) is similar to Santa Clara in some ways since this is a university town. Everything revolves around the students," he says.

*Update: Among former Santa Clara players overseas this season are Berkeley native John Bryant, in Germany; D.J. Mitchell in The Netherlands; and Tony Lewis, in Switzerland. Mitchell ended his college career at Texas A&M, per eurobasket.com.*

# Basketball a Global Game for La Salle Alums

*This story originally ran in the alumni magazine of La Salle in 2005 and is reprinted by permission.*

R asheed Quadri was born in Nigeria, grew up in England and went to high school in Boston. Now, after a four-year hoop career at La Salle, the 6-foot-3 point guard is in his first season as a pro in Hungary's top league. He plays for BC Marc Kormend, which has one of the strongest traditions for basketball in the central European country.

"I am loving it. It is like a dream come true. It is like a new beginning," said Quadri, die day before he began his European career. "I never thought I would be in Hungary playing, and I am closer to home." (He still has family in England.) The dream of playing pro basketball has come true for other former La Salle standouts.

While they may not be in the NBA, former Explorers who began this season with pro teams overseas, according to eurobasket.com, include Reggie Oleosa (Germany), Paul Burke (Germany), Mike Gizzi (Italy), K'zell Wesson (France), Milko Lieverst (Netherlands), and Victor Thomas (Argentina).

"You have to adjust your game. The players are better here," Okosa said of Germany's top league. "They say it is the third or fourth best league in the world. Everyone can shoot the ball. It is a lot faster (with a :24 clock). It is 100 times faster" than the American college game.

Okosa, who is several credits shy of graduation, averaged 11.3 points per game for La Salle in 2001-02 in his last college season. Burke, who averaged 15.6 points per game for the Explorers in 1994-95, averaged nine points per game last season for Oldenburg, Germany.

Gizzi, in his last college season in 1997-98, averaged 16.2 points per game for La Salle and averaged 23.4 last season for Patti in Italy. Wesson averaged 14.5 points per game in 2003-04 in Italy. In his last season for the Explorers in 1998-99, he averaged a whopping 10.8 rebounds an outing.

Lieverst, who is from The Netherlands, played at La Salic from 1987 to 1992. He averaged 5.0 points per game last season for a team in Amsterdam. Thomas averaged 19.7 points per game for La Salle in 2000-01, and scored 23.4 points an outing last season for his team in Korea.

Quadri, besides his global resume, also shows that you do not need impressive college statistics to play overseas. The most points he averaged in a season at La Salle was 4.9 per game as a sophomore and junior, and, last year, he averaged 4.6 points and 2.4 rebounds with 22 assists for the Explorers. He was second on the team in three-point shooting accuracy.

"You have to keep going. Nothing is going to be given to you," he said of playing in a foreign land. Quadri graduated last spring with a degree in management information systems. So did he pursue a job with a professional team in the U.S., such as the United States Basketball League or the Continental Basketball Association. "The opportunity in the minor leagues in the States did not present itself," said Quadri, who is getting to play point guard for his team in Hungary. "I am just glad to be playing."

Quadri, 24, drew attention last summer at a prestigious camp in Treviso, Italy. That helped lead to the job in Kormend, which began the season at home Oct. 23.

Like most former NCAA players in Europe, Quadri is provided, at no charge, an apartment and car bv the team he plays for. His main expenses are limited: long-distance calls and meals.

Okosa said his team in Germany provides him a car and apartment. Hungary allows two American players per team in its top league, and most of the 14 teams use the limit. Most European leagues allow no more than two Americans per team.

Quadri does not count as an American due to his background in Nigeria and England. Himgary is about the size of Indiana and has a population of around 10 million people. So what are Quadri's goals in hoops? "I am going to go as high as I can," Quadri said.

"If I keep improving, everything else will take care of itself " Paul Burke, 32, graduated from La Salle in 1996 with a degree in special and elementary education. Since college, he has played pro hoops in Sweden, England, Italy, Spain, and now Germany. "I never even thought about basketball as a pro career," he said in late October, while riding on a bus with his German team to a game. "I had some offers in baseball. actually, but I had an injury; I separated my shoulder my junior year."

Burke was almost drafted out of high school by the Cincinnati Reds, but he told them he wanted to attend college. He played two years of baseball for the Explorers and was a shortstop. "I was pretty lucky that I went to Sweden," he said of his first pro hoop season. "They are very western. Everyone pretty much spoke English. By far, Spain is the best place I have played. The Spanish league teams would beat any Atlantic 10 team."

Burke met his future wife, Nina, when he played in Sweden, and they were married in 1997. She is Swedish and they have two children, and live in Germany during the season.

*Update: Quadri ended his overseas career in Israel in 2007-08. Former Explorers who were active in Europe/overseas this season included Steve Zack, who played for the Sweet 16 team at La Salle in 2013. He has played in Latvia, Bulgaria, Poland, Turkey and Spain and went back to Israel in November, 2021 to play. Jerrell Wright of Philadelphia ended his college career in 2015 with the Explorers and has played in Austria, Hungary and France and was averaging nearly 16 points per game for a team in Japan in December, 2021.*

# Pandemic Had Impact in Germany

*This story originally appeared in the Daily News-Record in Harrisonburg, Virginia, in 2020 and was reprinted by permission of the publisher.*

In the midst of a pandemic, it has been a struggle for college basketball games to be held in some parts of this country. In Virginia alone, a few of the men's programs to pause due to virus concerns include James Madison, Virginia and George Mason. On the women's side, the Dukes and Richmond have had schedule snafus.

"The challenges keep rolling in," JMU men's coach Mark Byington said this week. Overseas, the obstacles have been there as well for several former Dukes who are playing in Europe and other regions. That is certainly the case for Jackson Kent, 26, a former JMU guard who was infected with the virus.

"Right now everything in Germany is locked down but my team is still playing," he wrote to the News-Record on Tuesday from Nuremberg, Germany. "We were all infected with corona a month ago and had to sit out for two weeks and now we are not playing our first game til Christmas because it is not safe to come back and play so quickly from what we were informed by our doctors. Overall, everything is going well despite the team getting corona a month ago. The league is doing quick tests before games now of every player and taking everyone's temperature."

Kent played four years for the Dukes and ended his college career in 2017.

Ron Curry, a former JMU guard, had his season delayed in Hungary due to protocol issues with his club, according to a spokesman in that central European country. His first game was Nov. 7 - he had 13 points on Saturday in a victory for perhaps the most storied club in league history in Hungary.

Other former Dukes overseas, according to eurobasket.com. at some point this season include Devon Moore in Germany, Juwann James (The Netherlands), Stuckey Mosley (North Macedonia), Alvin Brown (Armenia), Andrey Semenov (Russia), and Thomas Vodonovich (Luxembourg).

"Europe is definitely a different experience," Curry said in 2019. "I have a lot of fun playing over here. Any time you get to play basketball it is a good opportunity. The fans in Europe are very passionate."

On the women's side, former Dukes now overseas includes ex-Turner Ashby standout Kirby Burkholder.

After playing part of the previous three seasons in Hungary, she scored 11 points in 21 minutes of action Sunday in her first game this season in the top Polish league. She is one of three Americans with the club in Torun, a city of about 200,000 people in the central part of Poland.

The other Americans on her team played in college for Louisville and Stetson.

"It's a good league," said Burkholder, whose agent is based in Brazil. She learned of the job opportunity in Poland on Dec. 7, signed a contract the next day and flew overseas late last week.

Kamiah Smalls is playing this season in Italy. She was drafted in the third round by Indiana earlier this season out of JMU and played in seven games in her first WNBA campaign.

Smalls had 16 points on Sunday as her team lost by 51 points to Venezia; Smalls is averaging 18.5 points in her first 11 outings this season.

"I finally felt like a lot of my hard work had finally paid off," Smalls told the News-Record after her WNBA debut. "It's just a blessing to still be able to play the sport I love. It just feels really good."

Jazmon Gwathmey, from Liberty High in Northern Virginia, was averaging 14.6 points per contest in her first eight games for Sesto in northern Italy. She had 11 points Sunday in a victory over Bologna. She was drafted by Minnesota of the WNBA in 2016 in the second round after a standout career at JMU.

On the men's side, James, who averaged 14.3 points per contest as a senior at JMU in 2009, has played in Ireland, France, Switzerland and Lebanon since then. He played 2019-20 in Lebanon and Switzerland and in September played two games for a team in The Netherlands.

Brown had 11 points Sunday and was averaging 10.6 points per contest in his first 12 games. The 6-foot-11 forward finished his college career at USC-Aiken after transferring from JMU.

Kent, a guard from North Carolina who turns 27 next week, averaged 13 points in his first five games this season in Germany. Moore averaged 11.4 points per contest in his first five contests.

Mosley averaged 15.3 points in his first four games but had not played since Nov. 18, according to eurobasket.com. As a senior at JMU in 2018-19, he scored more than 16 points per outing and was a second-team all-CAA player.

Curry, 28, is a product of Paul VI High in New Jersey. He was also an all-CAA guard for the Dukes and ended his college career in 2016. He played in Germany, Latvia and Slovenia before heading back to Hungary for a second straight season.

"You have to be open and be mentally strong," Curry said of playing overseas. "You have to keep fighting and remember why you are here."

*Update: High Point, North Carolina native Kent averaged 11 points per game in Germany during the 2020-21 season. Smalls was playing for a team in Poland this season and averaged nearly 17 points per contest in her first seven games in the Polish league and 19.7 points per game for Lublin in the first two EuroCup contests.*

# Delaware Grads Saw the World

*This story originally ran in the alumni magazine at Delaware in 2008 and was reprinted by permission.*

Greg Miller, BE '01, did not have road trips like this when he played for the Blue Hens.

He and his current teammates recently made a journey of more than six hours to a basketball game in the German capital of Berlin. Not only did the former UD player have to travel across the heartland of Germany, but there ended up being a return trip that same night.

"Nobody is renting hotels in Berlin. We get back on that bus and head back home right after the game," notes Miller, who graced Delaware's hardwood from 1997-2001.

Welcome to life in the third division of German pro basketball. In his most recent season, Miller was averaging about 18 points and 2.5 assists per game, playing for the Proveo Merlins club in Crailsheim, a town of about 35,000 residents an hour east of Stuttgart in the southern part of the country.

"It's cool. It reminds me of college, since it's so small and everybody knows me," says Miller, who is spending his third season with Crailsheim and his sixth playing in Europe. "We're the main thing to do in town on Saturday. We get about 1,000 fans, and they have a good time."

Miller is one of several former Blue Hen basketballers who have kept their hoop dreams alive by going overseas to play for pay. On top of continuing to play basketball for a living, the former Delaware students get a chance to see other parts of the world while following the bouncing ball.

Jamal Basit, BE '01, a former teammate of Miller's at UD (where he was known by his given name, Ajmal), has played seven seasons as a pro in Germany. In addition to Basit and Miller, other former Blue Hens playing overseas as 2008 began included Mamadou Diouf, CHS '02, in Japan; Kestutis Marciulionis, BE '00, in Spain; Harding Nana, CHEP '06, in Poland; and Ndongo N'diaye, BE '02, in Syria, according to [www.usbasket.com], a Web site that tracks players and news of professional basketball worldwide.

On the women's side, Arek Deng, AS '06, is in England and Tyresa Smith, CHS '07, played briefly in Russia before leaving in December 2007 for the WNBA Detroit Shock. Former UD star Tiffany Young, CHS '05, played in Germany during the 2005-06 season.

Other recent players from the UD women's program to play overseas include Allison Trapp, AS '04, current UD assistant coach Tiara Malcom, CHEP '05, and Cindy Johnson, AS '01, who played in Iceland and Spain earlier this decade. They are among several standouts who starred for the Hens under Head Coach Tina Martin and Associate Head Coach Jeanine Radice.

Trapp played four seasons overseas after graduating from UD with a degree in history.

She split her first season abroad between Israel and Luxembourg, played her second year in Turkey, her third year in Greece and her final year, 2006-07, again in Turkey.

"Initially I went to Israel, and it was a huge culture shock" because of the dangers of war and terrorism, Trapp says. "You go into a supermarket, and they pat you down. It took a lot of getting used to. But if you can play for Coach Martin, you can do anything."

She had the chance to play overseas in 2007-08, but her father died recently and Trapp says she wanted to be closer to her mother in Philadelphia.

Malcom, who earned a degree in family and community services, now has completed two seasons as an assistant coach for UD. As a player, she overcame a partial hearing loss to become a four-year standout for the Blue Hens, where she was a three-time all-CAA selection and the league player of the year in 2005. Malcom scored 1,545 points at Delaware and set a school and CAA record with 535 free throws made.

The Wilmington, Del., native played professionally during the 2005-06 season in Barreiro, Portugal, with the GD ESSA Basketball Club.

"After we played our last game [at UD], Coach Martin gave me a list of agents," Malcom says. "I went through it with my parents. Once I got my agent, he shopped me to teams."

Malcom attracted attention from teams in Sweden and Israel, but she decided to play in Barreiro, a town about 20 minutes from the capital of Lisbon. She had not been overseas until she went to Portugal, where she became a tourist as well as a professional athlete.

"It was such an adjustment for me," she says. "It was so different. I saw a lot of castles in Portugal."

Johnson, another athlete who has since returned to the United States, is now splitting her time between Virginia, where she has an AAU and sports training business, and Utah, where she is working on a 104,000-square-foot sports training facility. She says she has good memories of her time playing abroad.

"Many people don't believe that I enjoyed myself while in Iceland," she says. "Although the cold was nothing I had ever experienced before, my location and teammates made my time there very enjoyable. I was less than five minutes from the Blue Lagoon and about 20 minutes away from Reykjavik, which is the capital city."

Johnson never made it to the WNBA, despite a few tryouts, but she seems to have few regrets.

"I appreciate everything that Tina and Jeanine did to help me experience post-graduate play. I am one that can actually say that I was afforded the opportunity to play at every level of the game," she says. "I think it has put me somewhat ahead of the curve."

Ahead of the curve is certainly not what all American players feel when they begin their pro careers in Europe. Upon his arrival in the Old Country in 2001, Miller had to deal with a new set of basketball rules, including a wider trapezoid lane, a 3-point line that's farther back from the basket and refs who monitor traveling much more strictly than in America.

The main problem, Miller admits, was the different style of play: "The style was more physical than in college. It's not American football, but you get held and pushed a lot."

His former Delaware teammate agrees. "It gets physical in the lane," says Basit, who says the major difference in Europe is the mentality, tactics and strategies of the game. "If we're leading by one point late, coaches here will foul the other team to have the ball for the last shot. Coaches in the States would never give an opposing team free throws to have the last shot."

Most North American players in Europe are paid a tax-free salary by their club and are provided free housing. Many top foreigners also are given the free use of a car and a meal allowance. Leagues in western Europe generally pay better than those in eastern Europe, with some of the best leagues found in France, Spain and Italy. Few American players venture to such countries as Romania or Serbia, where most teams cannot afford North American imports.

Miller and Basit have faced each other on three occasions during their time in Germany, including twice in the 2002-03 season. Miller, now playing in the same country as Basit, says he is continually amazed at how small the basketball world is.

"One and a half years before that first meeting [against Basit in Germany], I was dropping passes into him at Delaware, and now I was jumping into him and trying to draw fouls," he says.

Still, despite the difficult adjustments to living and competing in Europe, Miller says there's one big compensation: "I'm still playing basketball and doing what I love."

*Update: Nana, after two years in Denmark, is now in his fourth season in Switzerland.*

# Tar Heel Legacy

*A version of this story is slated to run in the alumni magazine of the University of North Carolina in 2022.*

San Sebastian, Spain — UNC graduate Taylor Koenen hustled after an offensive rebound, then fired a pass to Michigan State product Jenna Allen. Her American teammate returned the favor, finding Koenen on the left wing and the former Tar Heel post player didn't waste the opportunity. Koenen buried a three-pointer - as she has done dozens of times from her prep days in Minnesota to four years in Chapel Hill.

But this season, the basketball journey for 2020 graduate Koenen has taken her to a small town of about 60,000 people in the northwest corner of Spain in Ferrol where she plays in the top pro league in the country.

"I didn't know much about overseas life so I got a very good agent who was highly recommended and has been around forever," said the 6-foot-2 Koenen, standing on the court after the Spanish league game in October. "Spain is obviously very highly respected so I was very excited to get a chance to play here. It is very cool that every night it is a dogfight."

The basket is still 10 feet off the ground but so much has changed for Koenen, whose pro career began in Switzerland just after COVID-19 shutdown the Tar Heels' season in 2020.

On this Saturday night in San Sebastian - a good seven-hour bus ride from Ferrol - a crowd of about 250 people is on hand for the opening tip in a small arena as nearby local residents enjoy themselves with an outdoor meal on Avenida de Madrid with the temperature in the 70s in late October.

Koenen, with tourists enjoying the city this night, has to prove her worth as an imported player.

"She is a great teammate; I am very happy with her development," Spanish coach Lino Lopez said of Koenen, who was averaging nearly 13 points per game in November.

There are some familiar tinges of home for Koenen.

Soon after her nifty 3-pointer in the second half, the sports staple "We Will Rock You" blared in the arena on the north coast of Spain. The home team was en route to a lopsided victory, and each basket was punctuated by a young man in a No. 22 basketball jersey banging a drum to the tune of the home team's "I-D-K" moniker.

"People may not know a lot about it," Koenen said of European basketball. "But they know I am a professional basketball player and that speaks for itself. It is a different type of grind over here. Sometimes we practice three times a day. I don't think many people fully understand what we go through over here. But the athletes are over here and respect each other and respect what we do: we know it's not easy. Games are hard; we are an ocean away from family and friends."

The two seasons of pro ball for Koenen have included dealing with the pandemic and an increase in the racial reckoning in her home country.

That hit home for Black athlete Tierra Ruffin-Pratt, a four-year standout for the Tar Heels who began her pro career in the WNBA with Washington in 2013. The Virginia native played for Los Angeles in the WNBA in 2019-20 and has also played in Israel, Turkey, Hungary, and Poland before joining a team near Madrid in the Spanish league for the 2021-22 season.

How much follow the racial justice movement in 2020 while with Los Angeles?

"I followed it a good amount as I was part of the Social justice council in the WNBA. I was able to be part of a lot of things that took place in the league. It was great to see the college athletes using their voices and their platform for change," she wrote in an email from Spain.

Other former UNC women who spent at least part of the 2021-22 season overseas included Janelle Bailey and Waltiea Rolle in Spain; Shayla Bennett and Stephanie Mavunga in Poland; and Petra Holesinska in Hungary.

While Ruffin-Pratt was in Los Angeles in 2020, Koenen was in her first pro season overseas.

"Last year was tough. I was over in Switzerland for eight or nine months - that is a long time to not see your family and loved ones," she said.

Even though she wasn't drafted by the WNBA, Koenen still has her sights set on the top pro league for women. She said she was asked to attend several WNBA training camps but her contract in Switzerland wouldn't allow that.

This season, she made sure her contract allowed for a chance to attend a training camp with a WNBA team in the spring of 2022 if the opportunity arises.

"That is my ultimate goal," she said of the WNBA. "I want to play at the top level here and go make an impact in the WNBA."

Koenen was overseas to begin her career while the racial justice movement took off after the murder of George Floyd in Minnesota.

"I know that a lot of my (former UNC) teammates were doing social protests and obviously they had my full support," she said. "They knew that I couldn't be there because I was overseas. I saw their comments on social media, and they have my support in that aspect."

Ruffin-Pratt knows what it is like to play pro ball overseas and in the USA.

"The biggest challenge by far playing overseas is being away from family for long stretches of time! It sucks that you miss holidays, birthdays, and family events. But it's a way to make a living for myself and my family while doing something that I love," she notes.

"I dreamed of being a professional athlete all of my life," Koenen said. "Everybody is following the WNBA now. UNC is highly respected. Our grads come back and talk about their experience." And now she has her own to talk about.

# University of Minnesota to Madrid

*A version of this story is slated to run in the alumni magazine at the University of Minnesota in 2022.*

Madrid — Minnesota graduate Leslie Knight, just minutes after a one-sided loss in the top Spanish basketball league, didn't have to time to sulk. Before a full house on a Saturday night here in Madrid, Knight had a big smile on her face as she signed autographs for young Spanish girls who also dream of one day in the country's top basketball league for women.

Knight, 35, a 6-foot-1 forward who graduated from Hopkins High in 2005, averaged nearly 14 points and six rebounds per contest in her last season for the Gophers in 2007-08 and she was named a second-team all-Big 10 performer.

After one season in a pro league in Switzerland, she switched to playing in Spain. After a few years in the second division, Knight proved her worth and moved up to the first division. She is now in her third season with Estudiantes, a team that plays its home games in an arena just off a tree-lined street just south of the famed stadium of Real Madrid.

Knight was the Eurobasket.comAll-Spanish LF2 forward of the year in 2020, a first-team performer that year and helped Estudiantes to a regular-season title. She most likely is the longest-tenured foreigner in the Spanish women's league and she recently took the time for an interview after a game and the next morning at a café in a historic neighborhood in Madrid.

DD: How did the University of Minnesota prepare you for living overseas and also playing at a high level of basketball?
LK: "Off the court, I would say I minored in Spanish and I took English as a second language courses and I took some Latin courses. I really, for some reason, liked the culture and learning about different countries. So, when I did have the possibility of coming overseas and I saw I had the potential to go to Spain I was so excited because I felt, wow, so – I forget my English – if I can kill two birds with

one stone I can continue playing basketball and continue improving my Spanish, which I never thought I would need in my real life.

In college, I was able to study abroad in Venezuela in 2006. Now I have gone back and talked to my junior high Spanish teachers and my Spanish is better than theirs.

DD: What is it like as a foreigner to have ingrained yourself in the Spanish culture where young girls want your autograph? Does your team take part in community service?

LK: "The autographs always make your day. It is so nice to see the young girls smile. The younger generation is learning English in school and they are so excited to say hello to you, to ask you a question and use their English. So that is really fun."

DD: While you haven't played in the WNBA, you have been able to play against several of them in Europe. What has that been like?

LK: "It is an honor for sure. You see them in the WNBA; it is honor because in college we are in the same age and nobody is in the WNBA yet. If you are able to score on them, if you are able to defend them, it really makes you feel good."

DD: How does the Spanish league compare to other leagues in Europe?

LK: The Spanish league is the most competitive league in Europe, supposedly. From what I hear from other players who have played in other countries, they would agree. The level is getting better every year.

DD: From my 15 years of covering basketball in Europe, many American men and women players jump around from country to country, looking for the best situation. You have been able to stay in one country for a long time, which is not typical?

LK: "To be honest, one side of me is jealous of country hopping – what an opportunity to able to go and live in all of these different countries and have this experience. I have friends who have gone from Spain to Istanbul to Belgium to Germany and Israel. That would be so cool – when in your life are you going to be able to live for seven months and understand what that country is like. But is also nice to stay in one country – my Spanish has improved so much. My husband, I met him here, I live here with him. I miss home dearly but I also have found beauty and happiness here as well."

DD: How long do you plan to play as a pro?

LK: "That's the big question. I am 35. I always think about this: if I was a guy, if I was a man, I would probably continue playing but I want to have a family and I would like to have children before I am 40 so my playing days are coming to an end. Physically, I think I could continue but life doesn't want for anybody. This could potentially be my last year on the court and then once basketball is over, that's another great question. I did a master's in organizational leadership thinking that one day I would go back to the States and do college coaching. If I could continue working for the club I am playing for now in some aspect that could interest me quite a bit."

# Vermont Star Ended Up in Spain

*This story originally ran on the website of the America East Conference in 2015 and was reprinted by permission.*

It has been 10 years since Taylor Coppenrath helped lead Vermont to the 2005 America East title and its upset win over Syracuse in the NCAA tournament. While that was clearly an epic moment in Vermont hoops history, the 6-foot-9 Coppenrath has created his own memories as a pro basketball player the past decade.

As the America East Playoffs are held this month, Coppenrath is among dozens of former student-athletes from the conference continuing their basketball careers as professionals overseas.

Not every former Division I standout can land in the NBA. And for those former America East players who head overseas, a side benefit to playing for pay is the cultural awareness that can be gained along the way. The former Vermont star has played in Italy and has travelled to play in Lithuania, France, Germany and Slovenia.

Now in Burgos in northern Spain, Coppenrath says it can get cold and snowy at times.

"It reminds me a little of Vermont," notes Coppenrath, 33, who grew up in West Barnet, Vermont. "The city is beautiful. They have a cathedral that is huge and a little river that goes through the city. The team provides me with an apartment and a car to use."

The three-time America East Player of the Year has become a fan favorite in Spain. One fan wrote an article about him for a local paper on his birthday a few years ago.

That is a long way from an earlier stint in Greece, where he was not the only American import who had to deal with the economic challenges of that country while also coping with the language barrier.

"The first few years were an adjustment because I played in Athens, Greece and it was difficult with the language barrier," according to Coppenrath, who was averaging about 12 points per game in late February. "I wasn't sure how long I would play after that year but every year I played I experienced different countries, languages and experiences with players that I am still friends with."

"Off the court was dealing with not getting my money my first year in Greece. Also a few other years I experienced problems with getting paid late, but better late than never," he added. "One thing I never enjoyed about playing professionally was the business part that takes away from the sport I love to play. (It) seems over here that no one is ever completely on your side. They always have their own agenda."

Vermont has other former student-athletes all over the globe with Joey Accaoui in Lebanon, Marqus Blakely in the Philippines, Chris Holm in Japan, Sandro Carissimo also in Spain, Clancy Rugg in Luxembourg and Candon Rusin in Slovakia. Brian Voelkel was slated to begin the season in Australia in March.

Several of those players were scoring in double figures in late February, with Blakely at 22 points per contest, Rugg at 18.1, Accaoui at 13.5, Rusin at 12.0 while Holm was pulling down 12.2 boards per contest for the Shiga Lakestarts in Japan

Albany has three members of its 2013 America East championship squad – which beat Vermont for the NCAA bid – who have been overseas. And they have been scattered, from Mike Black in Bulgaria to Gary Johnson in Japan to John Puk in England. Being a long way from home is nothing new for Puk, who left his hometown in Iowa to play college hoops in upstate New York.

Another former Great Danes standout still playing is two-time America East Player of the Year, Jamar Wilson. Wilson, 31, currently finds himself Down Under playing in Australia playing for the 36ers.

He was drafted by Albany of the USBL in 2007. So, what is the biggest challenge on and off the court of playing pro hoops overseas?

"Being professional and coming to work every day," according to Wilson, a 6-1 guard. "There is no opportunity for you to show up to practice and not bring it. The season is 8-10 months; there is no room for sick days. Every day is a new day and like any other job trying to not let it affect your personal life. The hardest part off the floor would easily be time management. We are taught how to manage our time in college but it's a different aura professionally. After training you are free to do whatever you want. Managing your food schedule, treatment and social life is very important. Getting these things out of whack can cause issues with your performance."

But despite the challenges he has embraced his overseas experience, which has included stops in Belgium and Finland.

"Life has been amazing," according to Wilson. "I am lucky to be able to travel the world with my wife and daughter doing what I love. Before my daughter was born my wife played professionally as well. We would spend our days off trying to do something productive as it's a bit hard with two professional careers. I have played in numerous countries. Wherever we go we try to suck up the culture as much as possible. At the moment we have been down in Australia. It is summer at the moment. We live on the beach and spend much of our free time on the beach."

So how did life in the AEC at Albany prepare him for pro ball?

"America East prepared me for pro career by producing great talent each and every game during my five years in conference," wrote Wilson. "I enrolled into Albany as a 150-pound 18-year-old who was trying to learn how to properly wash my clothes and sent me away as a confident 23-year-old with a degree and direction in life. Will Brown and the coaching staff prepared me to be a professional throughout my time and still to this day. I still hear from coach at least once a week. When I need direction he always has the right input. Albany has a culture of preparing students to succeed after school in whatever you chose to do. Purple (family) is something we say and what we believe in. We are a family and we stick together no matter where we are in the world."

Tommy Brenton played at River Hill High near Baltimore before heading to Stony Brook. He is now in his second season in Japan.

"Living in Japan is very rewarding," wrote Brenton, who graduated from Stony Brook in 2012 and then got his master's degree the following year. "I love traveling and being able to see things I would never have the opportunity to without basketball. In my free time I like to visit the many historic shrines and temples located all over Japan. I live one hour north of Tokyo so I often spend my off days there. Tokyo is an amazing place with so much character and energy. In my contract the team included an apartment, car, cell phone, internet on top of my monthly salary."

Brenton says the top league in Japan allows three foreigners per team but at most two on the court at the same time. Some European leagues have similar rules.

"With company teams like Toyota, Toshiba, Mitsubishi, Hitachi the league is very competitive," he added. "Teams have very big budgets and recruit top division I players. Players that have been drafted or made NBA rosters are all over the league. I love those games most because my competitive nature comes out and I can see how I measure up."

Brenton says the coaching staff at Stony Brook helped him with his work ethic and mental toughness. "Every practice and every game is a test. You can be cut at any time and another player is waiting at home to take your spot. This isn't just basketball anymore it's a business and I plan to stay," he said of pro ball.

*Update: Coppenrath retired in 2015 after playing several years in Spain. Daniel Giddens, a former standout at Vermont, was with a team in Switzerland to begin this season.*

## UMass Product Visited Barcelona

*This originally appeared in the Springfield Republican in 2011 and was reprinted by permission.*

Ricky Harris, the former University of Massachusetts basketball standout, ran up and down the floor Tuesday afternoon on a day the temperature reached nearly 100 degrees in the Washington suburbs. He spent nearly one hour going one-on-one in full-court workout sessions against such former Division I players as Reggie Holmes (Morgan State), Devin Sweetney (St. Francis,

Pa.) and Mike Anderson (VCU).

Harris and his peers, several from the basketball-rich Baltimore-Washington corridor, worked out under the direction of trainer Joe Connelly, who has provided instruction to NBA players such as Roger Mason (New York Knicks), Hamady N'Diaye (Washington Wizards) and former Maryland star Juan Dixon.

"He is well respected. He knows how to put confidence in his players," said Harris, who first met Connelly when he was a freshman at Calvert Hall in Baltimore.

Harris, 23, is putting in long hours at the Laurel Boys & Girls Club in an effort to improve his shot at signing a contract to play pro basketball somewhere this coming season.

Last season, the 6-foot-2 combo guard played as a rookie pro in Lithuania and Ukraine. He averaged 7.3 points per game in eight Lithuanian League contests with BC Siauliai and 12.6 points per contest in five EuroCup games with the club.

"What impressed me about Ricky overseas last season was that he took on that point-guard role as well," Connelly said. "At UMass, he was a scorer. If he can learn to run a team (at the point), he may have a shot at the NBA."

While he would have loved to have joined former Minuteman teammate Gary Forbes in the NBA, Harris was glad for an opportunity to play in Lithuania. Luke Bonner and Chris Lowe, who also played at UMass, were with teams in Lithuania last season as well.

"That was the best available place for me," Harris said. "It is all basketball. Lithuania is a basketball country. They have a lot of talent in that country. They eat, drink and sleep basketball. You get a lot of love and appreciation there."

He then joined Ferro-ZNTU Zaporozhye in January in the Ukraine league and he averaged 9.9 points, 2.0 rebounds and 3.4 assists.

"The first month, I think I was homesick," he said. "I missed my mom. She was not able to come over. But my teammates and coaching staff, they all made me adjust and feel at home. I got used to it. After the first month, I think I adjusted pretty well."

Harris also was able to visit Spain, Montenegro, Estonia and Poland while playing in Europe, and he said the highlight was being in Barcelona.

He said the game was more physical in Europe, and Harris noted there are different rules overseas. For example, traveling is called if a player does not clearly put the ball on the floor before he picks up his pivot foot. Also, the ball can be touched within the cylinder without it being considered goaltending.

Most Americans with Division I experience get the free use of a car and an apartment in western European leagues, and many times their salary is not taxed by the host country. Top leagues in France, Italy, Spain and Russia pay NBA-caliber players six-figure salaries.

Harris said he was one of three Americans on his team in Lithuania and one of five Americans on his squad in Ukraine.

As of July 12, Harris had yet to sign a contract for the coming season. Harris said the NBA lockout could limit the number of jobs available overseas if those spots are taken by proven NBA players.

One NBA player who plans on heading to Europe for the coming season is Deron Williams, the All-Star guard for the New Jersey Nets who signed Saturday with a team in Turkey.

"Now I am waiting to see what happens," said Harris, after working out against Holmes, Anderson and Sweetney. His agent is looking into jobs with teams in Turkey, France, Cyprus and Ukraine.

Harris, a Baltimore native, ended his prep career at The Winchendon School in Massachusetts after he played at Calvert Hall in his hometown. He averaged 18.2 points per game as a sophomore for the Minutemen in 2007-08, when he was named Most Improved Player in the Atlantic 10.

*Update: Harris last played in South America during the 2019-20 season. Unique McLean, who played at UMass before transferring to St. Francis of New York, was playing in Finland to begin this season.*

# Afterword

Seville, Spain — Danny Agbelese, wearing flip-flops, sweats and a T-shirt, walked gingerly from his car in the parking lot to the arena that seated about 9,000 fans just south of downtown Seville in southern Spain.

The 6-foot-8 Agbelese played in college at Hampton in Virginia and since 2012 has played for pro teams in Uruguay, Iran, Italy, France, Greece and now Spain. He had 13 points and eight rebounds in just 17 minutes off the bench for Real Betis in a loss on Dec. 5, 2021 to Unicaja in the top Spanish league. He was born in Washington, D.C. in 1990.

It was late October of 2021, and Agbelese was one of four Americans with a team in La Liga ACB – the top league for men in Spain. Real Betis, the team sponsor, had lost six games in a row and Agbelese was

*The author (left) with Danny Agbelese before a practice session in Seville, Spain in October 2021.*

playing just a few minutes per game off the bench.

He had played the previous season in Greece, and told me he traded the chance for more playing time in that country in order to face better competition in the Spanish league. But there was another reason, perhaps: Greece is infamous for sometimes being late with a paycheck to foreigners, including Americans.

"That's Greece," said the powerfully-built, 6-foot-8 Agbelese, 33, who played in college at Hampton with overseas stops in Uruguay, Iran, Italy and France.

"They were always about two months late with pay almost every single time," Baltimore native Eric Atkins, a former point guard at Notre Dame, said of the season he played in Greece in 2014-15. "Now that I am removed from it, I can smile about it. At the time it wasn't pretty."

My wife and I were visiting Spain for two weeks late in 2021 (we were vaccinated and followed all of the travel protocols for plane, train and cabs) and I had contacted the press representative for Real Betis, Jesus Manuel Fernandez, about interviewing Agbelese for a newspaper in Washington, D.C. I had read that Agbelese was from the D.C. area and had played at college in Virginia before his overseas career began in 2012.

It turns out, after I spoke with Agbelese, that he attended the same French immersion school in Bladensburg, Maryland, that our two daughters attended before we headed to Hungary. And there is a good chance he was there at the same time as our oldest daughter, who is two years younger than Agbelese.

His parents moved from Nigeria to Maryland before he was born, and Agbelese is able to speak their native language. But he said picking up French didn't go so well. "Me and languages don't get along so well," he said.

That was something I could relate to, after taking Basic Hungarian at least two or three times at the Hungarian Studies Department at the University of Szeged.

With the pandemic a major challenge in 2020, Agbelese estimated that he was tested perhaps 100 times during the 2020-21 season in Greece. His story of late payments in Greece remained of an American who was playing in Europe years earlier, and said it took weeks for the heat to work properly at his apartment during the winter season.

Among the common questions from basketball fans about hoops in Europe is how much can Americans make overseas and what happens after there playing days are over.

The pay can not only vary from country to country but from club to club within a country.

And the disparity in pay between men and women in Europe is similar to the conditions in the NBA and WNBA, according to several American women.

In Hungary, one would think that capital Budapest would draw the top foreign players, right? But that has not been the case, with a much-smaller city (Székesfehérvár, know to locals as White Castle) about one hour west – the hometown region of former Hungarian NBA player Kornel David – having the resources for at least two decades to attract top American players.

When we arrived in Szeged in 2003, the men were in the B league in Hungary and didn't have any North American players. But at the start of the 2021-22 campaign, Szeged had three Americans, a Serbian and Australian on the roster. According to a spokesman with the Hungarian league, Szeged moved up to the highest level in 2010-11, with a textile company as the sponsor. Szeged finished third in the Hungarian league in 2020-21 with American Darrin Govens, a former standout at Saint Joseph's in Philadelphia. That led to the first Euro Cup appearance in history of the Szeged men.

The Americans in Szeged early this season were Justin Alston (Boston University), Tayler Persons (Ball State) and Keandre Cook (Missouri State), while Aussie Jesse Hunt played at Eastern Washington and was part of the Big Sky Conference finalists in 2018 and 2019. But the Szeged coach resigned earlier this season and later took a job with a team in Serbia – showing that mid-season changes can happen in Europe, just as it does in the NBA or with a major college program: see Maryland and Mark Turgeon in December.

An influx of cash can transform a pro team in nearly every country in Europe. And Americans, who are rarely role players overseas, see that in various ways.

Craig Ponder, who is from Bluefield, West Virginia, played in college at UNC Wilmington and then in 2016-2017 for a team in Reading, England. He said Division I American products "can easily make six figures per year" in countries such as Germany, Russia and Austria.

And for NBA-caliber players? "Some of those dudes can make a million dollars a year" in some western European leagues, said Ponder, now an assistant coach at his alma mater.

One of those players doing just that is Dez Wells, who was a teammate with Ponder in a post-graduate season at Hargrave Military Academy in rural Chatham, Virginia. From there Wells starred at Xavier before he ended his college career at Maryland. Since then, after being released by the Oklahoma City Thunder in 2015, the North Carolina native has played in Greece, Italy, the Philippines and China.

Wells averaged 37.1 points per game, per eurobasket.com, in eight games in the Governor's Cup in the Philippines in 2019 and was scoring more than 30 points per contest in China in his first 40 games for a team in China this season.

There are only so many spots in the NBA – that hit home for Ponder long before it did for some Division I products. He entered Hargrave with five players headed to high-major programs. One of them was P.J. Hairston, who starred at North Carolina and played in the NBA for Charlotte and Memphis.

"Coming out of high school, I didn't get the Division I offers I wanted," he said. "I was put on a pedestal my whole high school career in West Virginia. Going to school with those guys, I had a revelation then: maybe I am not as great as I thought I was."

One of his coaches planted the idea of going overseas to be a successful pro. And that was his mindset when he headed to Wilmington.

"The NBA is probably not where I will end up when this thing is all said and done," Ponder told himself in college.

The idea of heading overseas was reinforced to Ponder by Brett Blizzard, one of the best players ever at UNC Wilmington, who had a long career in Europe from 2003-19, mostly in Italy.

"He would come home in the summer and open up his gym," Ponder said. "All of us would pick his brain, him and (fellow star) Chad Tomko. They would give us the rundown if they thought we could play over there."

Tomko, a native of Virginia, played in Luxembourg and Spain after earning all-CAA honors in college. While many former Americans return from Europe to become coaches, Blizzard is one who went in another direction – he is now involved in real estate.

Chris Monroe, the all-time scoring leader at George Washington University, played for several years overseas, with stops in Hungary, Italy, France, Greece and Russia. He is now the associate director of development at GWU.

The thought of going overseas for Atkins began when he was a sophomore at Notre Dame. By his senior year, that took on more fruition as he saw limited chances for third-string point guards in the NBA.

"You can make more money in Europe than a third-string guard in the NBA," Atkins noted. Both current assistant coaches had to adapt overseas – on and off the court.

While in England, Ponder would sometimes "have to put the ice in the bath myself" for a post-game relaxer, he said.

That was a long way from college when he worked with Drew Moore, who is now with the Boston Celtics as an athletic trainer/performance therapist. Moore joined the Wilmington staff in 2014 as an athletic trainer.

Now Ponder is back in the United States and his players at UNC Wilmington have access to therapists and academic support staff.

Many former Americans who go overseas are able to make the transition to coaching, while others use their college degrees to enter the business world.

Sherman Rivers, a standout guard in college at William & Mary, is now a varsity head coach at a high school in Virginia. He played in England, Switzerland, Portugal and the Czech Republic.

Duane Simpkins had the distinction of playing in the U.S. for two Hall of Famer coaches – Morgan Wooten at DeMatha Catholic High in Hyattsville, Maryland, and Gary Williams at the University of Maryland in College Park. Simpkins played for pay in China, Italy, the Dominican Republic, France and Belgium and is now an assistant coach at George Mason University in Virginia.

Darris Nichols was a standout at West Virginia University and after ending his career in 2008 he played for one season in Hungary. After working as an assistant coach at Wofford, Northern Kentucky, Louisiana Tech and Florida, he became the head coach in his native Radford, Virginia, for the Division I Highlanders in 2021.

After playing in Greece, Atkins was briefly with a team in Hungary in 2015 before heading back to the United States to play in the D-League with the Idaho Stampede.

"I was so frustrated with the Hungary situation; I was ready to come home. I took the first thing that was available coming home," said Atkins, who was with Falco KC in the western part of Hungary. "The head coach didn't speak any English; we didn't see eye-to-eye. They started to tell me the wrong times for practice. In Hungary, you better be scoring" as an American import.

Atkins said his coach in Hungary was a former point guard who wanted a player at that position to score more. "That wasn't my style; I always tried to get my teammates involved," said Atkins, who averaged more than five assists per game in his last two years with the Irish of South Bend.

Now as an assistant, he can pass onto players at George Washington not only his experience at a Power 5 school such as Notre Dame but also the challenges, and rewards, of playing overseas.

"I really enjoyed my time in Greece, looking back at it," said Atkins, an all-ACC honorable mention player in 2014. "I was really open about what I wanted my coaching career to look like. That began with my Notre Dame coach, Mike Brey, when he started recruiting me in high school. I kind of always knew I wanted to (coach) and keep that thought in his brain. I was always taught to be very respectful with every coach that I talked that. I think on the backside of things that helped me."

Atkins said he had to educate family and friends about basketball in Europe.

"The common misconception was that the players weren't as good" overseas, he said. "And the talent level isn't up to par with what college was or even though it is pro it isn't really high level. People see the funky jerseys (in Europe), which now the NBA is adopting, which is funny to see. They see those things and it looks a little funky. Some people, their first thought is it isn't real or competitive (in Europe). But it is all that and more. When my mom visited (in Greece), she was blown away, blown away with the response from the fans and how passionate they are, which is amazing to see. I didn't know that" before heading overseas.

Another current Division I assistant is Ohio State's Tony Skinn, who grew up in Maryland and played in several European countries. He was a starting guard on the George Mason team that made its magical run to the Final Four in 2006.

While Atkins and Skinn appeared in March Madness, so did Galin Smith.

He scored two points in four minutes off the bench for Maryland in a 96-77 loss on March 22, 2021 to Alabama at Bankers Life Fieldhouse in Indianapolis. That came two days after he saw seven minutes of playing time and scored a single point in a first-round win over Connecticut.

A few weeks later, Mississippi native Smith was headed to Sweden to begin his pro sojourn. So, will the average Maryland fan ever hear or think of Smith again? Die-hard followers can keep up with him through social media or websites, but that is not the norm as some former players fall off the map – pun intended.

"The NBA is definitely still a dream of mine," Smith wrote to me in December of 2021 from Sweden. "Accepting the process of having to be overseas and working every day to achieve it is part of the journey that will make it even better in the end. With it being so cold and I'm having to adjust to that part I'm usually calling back home talking to my family or watching some of my favorite movies, shows, and podcasts."

He is provided with team gear, an apartment and meals every day of the week. That allows for him to focus on the task at hand – being a first-year pro, albeit thousands of miles from his American roots.

"I feel like one of the biggest misconceptions is the level of competition. Some of the best players from the U.S. along with Europe are competing here to either achieve the same dream or move themselves up to a higher club," he wrote.

In his first seven games in Sweden, the 6-foot-9 forward averaged about seven points and four boards per contest.

He was playing for perennial Swedish power Södertälje, a town of about 70,000 people near the Baltic Sea where there are records of people living in the region in about 4000 BC. That is the hometown of former tennis star Björn Rune Borg, who won 11 Grand Slam titles but never the U.S. Open.

One day, like Borg, Smith will have to hang up his athletic uniform.

"After my playing career I would like to either get into work with my degree in kinesiology as well as accumulating land and using it for financial gain," Smith wrote.

Deon Thompson played for an Elite Eight team at North Carolina in 2007 and later that summer was with the U-19 U.S. team that played at the world championships in Serbia. One of his teammates was Steph Curry, who had just finished his freshman year at Davidson. "He is a great player. He has a great presence inside," Curry told me of the 6-foot-9 post player from California back in 2007.

Jerry Wainwright, the coach of the U.S. team in Serbia, told his team about the history of the Balkan Wars in the 1990s. "He said we bombed them and people could be hostile toward us" at the event, Thompson told me then.

The Americans lost to Serbia in the gold medal game, even with Curry, Thompson and Tajuan Porter, a guard from the University of Oregon.

"This may be of one of greatest lessons in mental toughness these kids will go through," said Wainwright, the former head coach at North Carolina Wilmington, Richmond and DePaul and a one-time assistant at Xavier, Wake Forest, Fresno State, Marquette and Tulsa.

While almost every hoop fans knows how Curry turned out, that may not be the case for Thompson and Porter. After playing for the Tar Heels through 2010, Thompson has played for pay in Greece, Slovenia, Germany, China, Turkey, Serbia, Spain, Lithuania, Puerto Rico and was back in Spain for this season with Zaragoza as of December. Porter played for pro teams in the U.S. and in France and Turkey and last played in Switzerland during the 2019-20 campaign.

Former Towson star Calvin Lee, after college, played in a pro league in the United States then headed Kosovo in eastern/central Europe for about three months in 2012. Kosovo was the scene of bloody battles during the Balkan Wars of the 1990s, something Lee did not know much about before he got there.

Gary Neal, another former star for the Tigers, played overseas in Turkey, famed Benetton Treviso in Italy and in Spain before signing a three-year deal with the Spurs of the NBA in 2010. That is not a typical path to The League, but a trip a few Americans have been able to navigate in the past two decades. Neal last played overseas in 2018-19 before returning to Towson as part of the coaching staff.

Many Americans who are not NBA-caliber such as Neal use countries such as Hungary as springboards to better leagues. That was the case for Terry Williams, who was a standout at Georgia Southern through 2005. His first year was in Hungary and he later played a few years in France before his career ended in 2015. Zack Bryant, who ended his college career at Georgia Southern in 2021, spent time in Germany and Finland this season as a rookie pro.

Williams told me during his season in Hungary that a coach told him early on about life overseas and about another American who didn't last long in Europe.

"He was a great player; but two days later (after being in Europe), the player went home," said Williams, who had a girlfriend back in the States at the time. "You have to focus. You can't worry about what goes on back home."

Americans over the past two decades have played at the Division I level with teammates from overseas, notably Europe. Then the same thing happens when the Americans play international ball after college. Zoran Viskovic grew up in Croatia and played in college at Valparaiso in Indiana earlier this century when the roster was flooded with Europeans under former coach Homer Drew. A 6-foot-11 post player, Viskovic had a long career overseas.

"Growing up in Europe helped me adjust to the European style of basketball, but playing four years in college was by far the best, pure joy of basketball," he told me. "Being European also helped me to adjust to all different cultures and places that I lived. Sometimes talking with U.S. kids that are going overseas, I get a feeling of them not being ready, or not knowing what to expect. I think Valpo does a great job of introducing foreign cultures to its students."

Meanwhile, the landscape for American women who head to Europe to play pro basketball has an added challenge – a huge disparity in pay.

And like American men, the women sometimes are paid late as well.

"Major money issues," former James Madison University standout Kirby Burkholder said of her time in Poland during the 2020-21 season. It took about seven months after she left to get caught up in payment.

And Burkholder, the daughter of my first cousin, is not alone among Americans who have to rely on foreign agents to find them the next landing spot. In her pro career, Burkholder has had four different agents – one American and three European.

Those challenges of overseas hoops paid off last fall when Burkholder signed to play with Athletes Unlimited, based in Las Vegas and slated to open the season Jan. 26, 2022. On social media, Burkholder announced the transition and pointed out it would be her first time playing basketball in the United States in nearly eight years.

The league will last for about a month for 44 players, with all of the games in Las Vegas.

"Athletes Unlimited provides American players an additional opportunity to play in the United States," Jantel Lavender of the Indiana Fever told espn.com. "I am also looking forward to the unique Athletes Unlimited format: every week a new team, playing with -- as well as against -- some of the best players in our sport. I hope it's something that can be an option for women's basketball players for many years to come."

When Burkholder was in Poland, there was a limit on just two Americans per team. In many European leagues for men, many times there are at least three or four Americans per squad.

"There are still more opportunities for men," Burkholder said.

American women can make as much as $1,000 Euros a month (about $1300 U.S. dollars) to $10,000 a month, according to a veteran of European leagues.

Most American players, men and women, are usually provided the free use of an apartment and many times the use of a car.

Another problem for WNBA-level players is that many of them don't have enough down time to let their bodies recuperate. To make a decent living, many women are forced to play in Europe in the winter after a summer in the WNBA.

The average pay for an NBA player during the 2020-21 season was about $7.5 million. The average, according to Yahoo Finance, for a player in the WNBA last season was about $120,000 with the top player making around $221,000. Steph Curry was the top NBA earner at $44 million during the 2020-21 campaign.

Since the WNBA season is only a few months long, and the pay a pittance compared to NBA superstars such as LeBron James and Curry, American women are all but forced to head overseas during the traditionally winter season for two seasons: to make a living and continue to face strong competition.

Burkholder said the same disparity exists between the pay of men and women overseas. "A men's player can make so much more," she said.

Most teams in Europe begin practice in August and the season may stretch until May or June, depending on the country. That has resulted in many over-use injuries for women playing in the WNBA and in Europe.

It's a sore point to many American hoopsters, even some whom never made the WNBA.

Leslie Knight, 35, who grew up in Minnesota, has played pro ball in Spain for more than a decade. She stayed at home to play in college at the University of Minnesota, then played in Switzerland her first season as a pro before switching to Spain in 2009. She has been there ever since, marrying a native of Spain and becoming nearly fluent in the local language.

She has seen much of Europe, but gender inequity is a sore topic with Knight as Title IX in the United States – promising fair treatment for women in sports – marks its 50th anniversary in 2022.

"I cannot imagine my life without sports," Knight wrote to me after we met at a café in Madrid in the fall of 2021. "Sports have been the center of my life ever since I was a little girl when I was running around and trying to do and be exactly like my two older brothers. I've always been a tall, strong female and being active, pushing the limits of my body and competing have been my day to day ever since I can remember. Staying fit and playing on a team make me feel good, mentally, emotionally and physically."

"My happiness and well-being stem from my sport and the friendships I've made over the years," Knight adds. "Literally, almost everything in my life is or was thanks to sports. To think of a life without weights, gym shorts, tennis shoes or teammates is impossible for me, yet when my mom was a little girl in the 50s nobody expected or thought she'd be an athlete. She was taught to cook and sew which are great qualities to possess and I am a firm believer that everyone should know how to cook, at least the basics, but there is more to life than cooking and sewing for everybody else."

"Thank goodness women fought for the right to participate in sports and be treated as equals. In today's world there are still differences between how male athletes are treated in comparison to their female counterparts and these differences frustrate me, sometimes on a weekly basis, but at least we get to play, travel and earn a living playing sports. There's still a lot of room for improvement, yes, and we'll have to continue fighting for our fair share of the pie. I am forever grateful to all the brave, courageous, outspoken women of the past and hope to add my efforts as well so that girls born today will grow up to see themselves respected, valued and treated just as well as their male peers," Knight continues.

"Honestly, this topic really gets my blood boiling. The way history has treated and viewed women continues to have lasting effects in today's society and it irks me beyond belief. I'm reading a book right now and it takes place in the 19th century. The things women could or couldn't do upset me as a reader and that was more than 100 years ago. Life has changed a lot since then but we continue to see inequality in the 21st century. Who have been making the rules for the last however many centuries? White men. Women aren't strong enough to play full court or to run marathons etc. etc. But who are you to say what I am capable of? Just because I was born female?

"Many times the differences are financial and possibly not a matter of being male or female, but why do the men tend to generate more profit? Because they have more marketing, they have more incentives, they've been playing the game longer than women have and therefore have a 50 year head start, they're given the best practice times, they're babied and everything is taken care of for them so that all they have to worry about is performing, they make more money and can dedicate all their attention to being the best they can be without thinking about dozens of other things that the majority of female athletes do have to think about," Knight concluded.

My entry into European basketball began in 2003 when my wife and our two daughters, then 11 and 9, moved to a university city just southwest of the famous Hungarian plains. Once we moved back to Maryland, both of our daughters played volleyball at separate high schools – one, Dani, went on to play at the Division III level in college while Katie was a student manager for the volleyball team at the University of Maryland.

A generation after moving to Hungary, my oldest daughter was just a few years younger than Knight – whose passionate response about the life of an American, and woman, overseas seemed like a fitting capstone to 18 years of following and learning about basketball and life in Europe. My hope from this book is that you, the reader, now know more about basketball in Europe and the joys and challenges of Americans who head there to fulfill their hoop dreams.

# Acknowledgments

My family, including my wife Liz and two young daughters, moved to Szeged in southern Hungary in the summer of 2003 without knowing a single person there.

The people I want to thank first are Hungarians who made us feel at home and much more. Many of them had little interest in basketball, and perhaps didn't even know there were some Americans playing pro ball in their country! No matter.

Among those who helped us get settled were colleagues of my wife at the university. That included Dr. Fenyvesi Anna and many others. (Hungarians write their family name first, then the first name).

They, also in turn, answered my questions about train travel in Hungary, knowledge that helped me connect with Americans with hoop teams scattered around a country that's about the size of Indiana.

Another big help was Dr. Szeghalmi Zoltán, a medical doctor I met with several times for coffee so he could practice his already solid English. A former national team soccer player in Hungary, Zoltan would translate for me when I brought him the daily sports newspaper in Hungary, with its basketball coverage. (I eventually learned a few Hungarian words that helped in reading the boxscores).

Other Americans living in Hungary at the time who greatly assisted our transition into the culture were Rob and Donna George, Lea and Doug Coppage, Chris Hayes, and Don Peckham. Their love of the people and culture of Hungary was and still is evident.

Fast forward 18 years and this book finally took form long after I had first considered it.

Thanks to two of my former editors at the weekly paper in Laurel, Maryland – Joe Murchison and Melanie Dzwonchyk – for their support. Joe put me in touch with Russell Nemec, whose graphic design work on the front and back cover of this book is superb. When I saw his rough draft, my first thought was: it will be all downhill for readers once they open the book. The cover is that good; hopefully, the stories were up to par.

A big thank you as well to page designer Crystal Graham of Augusta Free Press in Waynesboro, Virginia. Crystal and her husband, Chris, a published sports author in his own right, have been very successful in their post-newspaper careers with their company.

It was gratifying to team up with a small company located just a few miles from where I grew up playing basketball in the driveway at the farm with my brothers, Daryl and Dennis, both of who played basketball in high school at Eastern Mennonite in Virginia. Hoops was a big part of our childhoods; my late farmer father, Dan, and my mother, Marilyn, a long-time educator who now lives in Bridgewater, Virginia, made sure we kept up with our schoolwork before those pickup hoops games took place.

Phil Kushin, a long-time friend, came to visit us in Hungary three times. He is also one of the best copy editors around, with a long stint at The Washington Post, and he assisted with the preface and foreword for this book and provided wonderful moral support along the way.

Of course, I can't leave out the scores of American basketball players I have interviewed over the past 18 years. They allowed me glimpses into their professional, and sometimes private lives, and I am grateful for that trust. One of them, former Mercer standout Ledon Green, was one of the first I connected with in Hungary and a few years later he invited me to his wedding to a local woman in Szeged at the famed dual-spired Votive church. I gladly accepted.

I also wanted to thank you for the congregations of Sion Church in Szeged and Washington Community Fellowship, our long-time church in the U.S.A.

Also, a huge thanks to Sports Information/Athletic department personnel who assisted in setting up interviews with former European players. That includes Kevin Warner and Jason Krech at JMU in my hometown of Harrisonburg and those nearer my adopted home in Maryland, including Kevin Burke at George Washington, Maureen Nasser and Mark LaFrance at George Mason, Diana Pulupa at Georgetown and Rose DiPaula, Sean Ellenby, and Keith Cameron Sneed at the University of Maryland. Thanks also to Joe Browning with the University of North Carolina Wilmington and Pete Clawson at William & Mary.

I thank and still mourn three of my writer friends who, sadly, are no longer with us.

Joseph White, a North Carolina native who worked in England early in his career, gave me the chance to do freelance work with the Associated Press in the 1990s; he was later named the AP sportswriter of the year, and sadly passed away in Virginia in 2019. Working NBA, MLB and NHL games with him was never dull.

I treasure the conversations about basketball I had with John McNamara, my colleague at a daily paper in Maryland in the 1990s. We spent some fun mornings playing pickup hoops with other sportswriters in Annapolis during that time. John had played basketball in high school in Washington, D.C. and he loved to kid me about my Virginia hoop roots – and how they didn't stack up with his alma mater, the University of Maryland. Tragically, John was killed in a shooting in the newsroom of The Annapolis Capital, along with four other journalists, in 2018. His widow, Andrea, completed and published John's book: "The Capital of Basketball: A History of DC Area High School Hoops" the following year and it is excellent.

Another friend, Jeff Seidel, wrote several sportsbooks while based in Baltimore, including those on the Orioles and Ravens, and was a good-sounding board over the years on many topics. Sadly, he passed away in August 2021.

Last, but not least, to thank is my family: my wife Liz, and our daughters Katie, and Dani. Our three years in Hungary were not without challenges, but I would like to think that time made us all better people, or at least more informed about the world. All three of them helped make me a better person and have enriched my life in many ways.

David Driver
Cheverly, Maryland
January 2022

# About the Author

David Driver is a native of Harrisonburg, Virginia and grew up in nearby Dayton. He played baseball for one year at Eastern Mennonite University before graduating in 1985 with a degree in English and a minor in journalism. Driver lived with his wife, Dr. Liz Driver, and two daughters in Hungary for three years and has interviewed American basketball players in more than a dozen European countries. A former sports editor of papers in Harrisonburg and Arlington in Virginia and Baltimore and Laurel in Maryland, he is a member of the  United States Basketball Writers Association. He also covered the Washington Nationals during their 2019 World Series season for The Washington Times. Driver is now the Communications Director for MVP International, an agency founded in Virginia that fosters overseas sports travel for high school students in various sports. Driver can be reached at www.daytondavid.com and @DaytonVaDriver.